cooking
— with —
cocktails

cooking

— with —

cocktails

100 Spirited Recipes

kristy gardner

The Countryman Press
A division of W. W. Norton & Company
Independent Publishers Since 1923

For information about permission to reproduce
selections from this book, write to Permissions,
The Countryman Press, 500 Fifth Avenue,
New York, NY 10110

For information about special discounts for bulk
purchases, please contact W. W. Norton Special Sales
at specialsales@wwnorton.com or 800-233-4830

Manufacturing through Asia Pacific Offset
Book design by Nick Caruso Design
Production manager: Devon Zahn

The Countryman Press
www.countrymanpress.com

A division of W. W. Norton & Company, Inc.
500 Fifth Avenue, New York, NY 10110
www.wwnorton.com

978-1-58157-397-8

10 9 8 7 6 5 4 3 2

A toast. . . . This book is written for anyone who's done shots with me, who will share a bottle of wine with me, and who imbibes good alcohol as much as they feast on damn good food. Most important, it's written for the dude who abides my bourbon habit, daily. As Julia Child said, "You are the butter to my bread, and the breath to my life."

Contents

Introduction   9

How to Consume This Book   15

cocktails 33

appetizers & bar snacks 59

soups & salads 81

meaty 99

fish & seafood 125

(mostly) vegetables 151

sweets 177

staples & sauces 215

Acknowledgments   239

Index   243

Introduction

This Is a Hard One . . .

I'm sitting here. Hidden away on one of the Gulf Islands, with my cup of Baileys and coffee and a simple omelet, thinking about how to start this book. I keep getting distracted by the crisp morning sunshine, wondering what'll be at the market for dinner tonight, and debating about whether I should put pants on.

Writing is hard.

Pants are hard.

Drinking Baileys and coffee in the middle of the forest with nothing but the birds to keep me company, not so damn bad.

I got to this place by accident. Not the Gulf Island; I drove here. I mean this place of creating a book of recipes that nourish and feed the people in my life. Hopefully now the people in yours, too. It's involved a lot of hard work, support from some really spectacular and generous people, and a bit of dumb luck. But it wasn't what I had planned for my life. I hadn't planned much, if I'm being honest. I hadn't got that far yet.

I didn't find cooking; cooking found me. You can say I kind of fell into it. Or if margaritas were involved—and at age twenty-five they usually were—I stumbled into it. Much like most of my romantic liaisons. No shame here, my friends, no shame.

My Origin Story
(not quite as dope as Batman's).

I grew up in a small town in Alberta of 5,000 people, where bumper skiing, Budweiser, and meat and potatoes were the norm. Parties were "down on the farm," cows grazed at the end of my street, and each night my parents, my brother, and I would sit down as a family to eat wholesome dinners. Mom regularly crafted pizza, pierogi, cakes, and cookies from scratch. When she was working late, Dad would assemble one of the three dishes in his culinary repertoire: meat loaf, liver, or spaghetti. We enjoyed home-cooked food, in a well-loved kitchen, in the middle of the Canadian prairies.

I left home at nineteen and lived in Calgary for six years, working off and on in various restaurants and bars, enjoying the social aspects of them and the wads of cash I'd walk home with every night. The main star at my dinner table during that time was take-out Chinese food and my infamous KD tuna casserole, which essentially consisted of a drained can of tuna stirred into a bowl of boxed mac and cheese and topped off with a healthy dousing of ketchup. I was a chef in the making! Or not.

A lot of great things happened during that time in my life. A lot of shitty things happened, too.

On a whim and a bottle of whiskey, at twenty-five I packed up and headed west—as do many wayward folks who don't know what the hell else to do. It wasn't until a couple of years after arriving in Victoria, British Columbia, that I was served the inspiration for what would become my passion for the next decade.

I enrolled in college and, in my second year, took a class called "Women, Food & Culture." It—and the no-BS professor who taught it—would forever change my life. Not to mention the lives of those around me. Have you ever invited a passionate and newly converted feminist to dinner? Yikes.

Once I discovered the politics of gender in our foodways and the issues in our food systems, and learned to love knowing where my food came from (that wasn't always an easy road), foraging at the farmers' market and coming home to cook that bounty became something I did daily, with pleasure. And usually with wine.

I also met the love of my life, who just so happened to be a patron of the bar I was working at, as well as a theoretical physics researcher at the university and a TV writer, all rolled into one. John was dreamy. And we relished dining together each night, just as I had with my family when I was growing up.

It was about this time I started working in a swanky restaurant that epitomized the kind of food I loved. Seasonal ingredients. Locally raised. Organically produced. Small plates meant for sharing. It also served good wine and made damn fine cocktails. I began to appreciate liquor for more than its ability to get me into trouble.

Time went by, and one weekend, John turned our home into a movie set—actors, producers, videographers, and their assistants took over every corner of our house. I promptly locked myself in the office (otherwise known as the "big" closet) and started a blog. It began partly as a distraction from the banging and clanging outside my little room and partly from passion—I wanted to document and share what I was learning in school with the world; I wanted to make it better.

Over the last six and a half years, *SheEats.ca* has morphed into a variety of different things, including a forum for real food advocacy, a farmers'-market-friendly recipe resource, and an opportunity to connect with people who like to eat and drink as lustfully as I do. But its central focus has stayed the same: Local. Seasonal. With booze. And the community around it has nourished me in ways I never expected. Both literally and figuratively. If you're part of that community and I haven't heard from you, I'd love to: kristy@sheeats.ca.

I don't know whether I succeeded in making the world better through the blog, but it and all those who have taken, do take, and will take the time to let me know they've made a recipe, commented on a blog post, or shared their love of good food and drink with me on social media or via e-mail have certainly made mine better. I'm surrounded by good and inspiring company and am grateful for it.

A few months ago I was contacted by Ann at The Countryman Press, asking whether she could commission my photographs for the covers of two books the company was publishing. She also asked whether I wanted to write one myself.

I was speechless—was this a dream? Was it real? I didn't know. A year later it seems it was, because now I've found my voice and get to share my very long-winded, roundabout story, bad jokes, and favorite recipes with you.

Sometime during my journey from small-town Alberta, where I thought a bottle of ketchup and dried pasta was the epitome of high cuisine, to this porch on Salt Spring Island, where I fumble to articulate what this book is truly about, mealtimes have become something more than just food—they've become an adventure. A story. A shared experience between the people who produce our food, the people at our tables, and ourselves. From the planet to plate to glass to tummy.

I believe the best memories—the ones that nourish us, touch our heart, and evoke spirited laughter from the deepest parts of our belly—are forged through good food and drink.

Put the two together, and you undoubtedly have a recipe for intoxicating deliciousness.

Not to mention wild stories for years to come.

And it often starts with an onion, an idea, a little courage, and a shot of tequila.

You Are What You Eat

If you're into really good food cooked from scratch with fresh ingredients, drinks with a little somethin' somethin', and enjoying what you put in your mouth, this book is for you.

Through these pages I'm inviting the hungry, life-loving, alcohol enthusiast in you to look to your bar for inspiration for your next meal.

This book begins with some helpful information about my kitchen and what you'll need to make every recipe here. You might not need everything—just whatever makes your life better and cooking process easier. If you can, buy your booze from artisan producers—many wineries, breweries, and distilleries sell directly to the consumer and that means more dolla' dolla' billz in their pockets to keep making great wine, beer, and spirits (rather than large stores or corporations). For food, I suggest you look to your farmers' market, community-supported agriculture (CSA) provider, and/or neighborhood butcher for ingredients, and shop locally in season for the best flavor and results in the finished dishes.

The recipes are broken up by meal course, starting with the bevvies. Obviously I end with some recipes for staples that you might wish to make a part of your kitchen repertoire. Most of the recipes have roots in Italian, Spanish, or French cuisine, but a few venture off the beaten path, asking you to endeavor on a scrumptious quest with me. To enjoy your meals with passion, with friends, and with alcohol.

A few dishes are childhood favorites that I've adulted the shit out of, while others are new ones that have been concocted along the way. Some are quick and easy (like me, ow ow!), while others take more care.

Most of them involve cheese or butter or bread or meat and lots of farm-fresh, locally seasonal produce.

None of them include reduced-fat or low-calorie ingredients. If you're concerned about those things, I say take everything in moderation. Move your body more than you watch TV. As Sarah Copeland says, "Eat cake and vegetables." Because life is better in whole flavor and full color.

All of them are both boozy in nature and delicious in flavor.

I can't promise you'll love every single recipe here. We all have different tastes. Thank sweet God for that. The world—and our plates—would be very boring if we didn't. And I encourage you to adjust recipes to your preferences; choose your own adventure! Be a badass in your own kitchen.

Speaking of badasses, Julia Child was kind of a badass.

The woman cooked with butter, finished with butter, and binged on life with enthusiasm. And I wholeheartedly agree with her saying, "The only real stumbling block is fear of failure. In cooking you've got to have a what-the-hell attitude."

I've made a lot of my life decisions with that perspective in mind—most of the ones I've just listed, actually. And now I've started this book with fear and hope and kind of a hungry belly (what else is new?). Thank goodness, I have that omelet. You've begun an adventure in your kitchen by picking up this book. So, what have you got to lose?

Pull up your big-girl pants (I'll go put some on), make some food, invite me over for dinner, and give 'em hell, kid.

Cook. Eat. Imbibe. Live. And repeat.

How to Consume This Book

I've never been much of a rule follower myself—break the damn things, I say.

But if you're going to make the recipes in this book or create your own, there are a few guidelines to follow for the most delicious success.

You don't have to follow these—you can just pop that cork and see what happens (story of my life)—but to save you frustration and confusion, and help you put the best food on your table, here are some suggestions about how to get it on in the kitchen.

BTW: You don't have to put your food on the table. I eat most meals with a plate balanced precariously on my lap.

Read the Damn Recipe

I'm impulsive. One of the biggest mistakes I make when I get a new cookbook or find a new blog is to give the recipes a cursory glance and then wing it. I miss important details, such as the fact that I don't have a key ingredient, or I haven't allocated enough marinating or resting time, or the short ribs weren't fall-off-the-bone tender because I didn't bring the pot of braising liquid to a boil before I put it in the oven. My biggest suggestion to you is to read the damn recipe—in its entirety—before starting. Twice.

Google That Shit

I want you to eat really delicious food. I know sometimes techniques or ingredients that you aren't familiar with can be intimidating. But if I can do it, you can do it. If you're unsure about something, Google it! So much useful information and tutorials are available online, there's no reason to say, "I don't know what that is." You've got this.

Season Everything

Salt, like searing and caramelization = flavor. So use it.

I don't list this in each and every recipe because it would be redundant, but please oh please, for the love of salt, season everything at every

stage of the cooking process and taste as you go. That way you can add more or stop altogether, so your food tastes the best that it possibly can.

We've developed an unhealthy aversion to sodium and I don't like it. Generally, if you cook from home and don't incorporate many processed ingredients/foods into your diet, you can season your food with salt and pepper adequately (I argue even generously) without fear of retribution from your circulatory system.

So, please, do your pleasure senses a favor and season season season.

Booze + Food

= yum, right?

All of the recipes you'll find here employ alcohol in their preparation in some way. Rarely does all the alcohol burn off when cooking, but 99 percent of the alcohol "burn" will, and you'll be left with flavors and aromas. Some recipes are heavier on the boozy taste; others use it more as an aromatic, contributing to the finished dish in its entirety, kind of like herbs or salt.

For the recipes where the alcohol clearly doesn't cook out, e.g., 3-Way Boozy Ice Cream (page 198), Fiesta Boozy Guac (page 232), Drunk Grilled Pear & Brie Salad (page 83), or any of the cocktails, you'll get a much stronger booze flavor than in something where it's used more sparingly, e.g., Vodka Spiked Butternut Squash "Parcels" & Bloody Mary Tomato Jam (page 74), Mom's Stout Baked Beans (page 164), or Margherita "Margarita" Pizza (page 155).

Be Judgmental

Cooking, mixing cocktails, and pairing the two together takes a bit of experimentation. You didn't get good at all the incredible things you do each day by its just happening. You worked at it. You practiced. You honed those skills. And baby, you got mad skillz!

The same is true for the kitchen.

You'll know if a dish is missing something or doesn't fit with your preferences. Maybe it needs more salt, a splash of citrus (my secret weapon), a dash of acid, a bit of sweetness, some fresh herbs, or simply another margarita down the hatch.

Perhaps your oven runs hotter than mine or you live in a different altitude or climate than I do—these things affect how food reacts to cooking and baking.

If you don't eat dairy or gluten or meat, you probably won't enjoy this book to its fullest. But make substitutions if the moment moves you. I can't speak to dietary restrictions because I'm fortunate enough to not have sensitivities, so I don't know enough to speak confidently to them. But you know your body. Your kitchen. Your home. And your alcohol tolerance.

These recipes are perfected to my tastes, so if you prefer less heat, more cheese, red wine over white, gin over vodka, or what-have-you, go for it! You won't know unless you try.

The more you cook and the more you mix, the better you get at it.

So, do it. Lots.

Use Quality Ingredients

I mainly cook and drink what's locally in season. For many reasons. And one of those is because the level of yumminess in my finished dish is entirely dependent on the quality of ingredients. And the quality of ingredients is contingent on their freshness and wholeness—both for flavor and nutrition.

So, shop locally in season for your vegetables, fruits, and grains from small-scale producers and farmers who raise food by practicing organic methods and without GMOs. Support your local winemakers, craft breweries, and small-batch distilleries when appropriate. Grow some herbs on a windowsill, if you can. Sign up for a CSA delivery program. Dive face-first into some wildflower honey. Eat full-fat, whole foods. And when it comes to meat and eggs, look for pasture-raised animals. Use Google to discover what's available in your area and make luscious use of it.

The best meals come from the best ingredients from pretty much the best place in the multiverse—our planet. So, while we take care of our belly and good company, let's take care of our home as well.

Also, I promise, that's the last time I'll mention nutrition in a book brimming with spirits, cheese, and carbs.

Some Thoughts on Pairing Food & Drink

I thought long and hard about whether to include a food and drink pairing guide in this book, showcasing the basic flavors of various spirits and how they match with what I've paired them with for each dish.

But ultimately I concluded the trouble with that is threefold:

1. **Every spirit is different, depending on the distillation and brewing process.**

What is exemplified in one gin may be completely different in another. And how do you cover an entire bar's worth of flavor profiles when the book is more about cooking with booze, not necessarily the alcohol itself?

2.   **There are plenty of experts who have covered that breadth of information in a way that this topic truly deserves.**

And they do it justice by detailing the culture of drink in its entirety, far more comprehensively than I can do in a book about cooking. They talk about bar setup, liquor history, differences, mixing technique, flavor profiles, and so on.

I cover a few of these things as the recipes call for it, but ultimately that kind of detailed information goes beyond the scope of this book.

If this is something you want to explore more (and you should—it's super-duper great fun), I have my own cocktail flavor bibles and I highly recommend you explore the bookstore for a cocktail-focused book that speaks to you.

3.   **When we cook, we learn by doing.**

Just as I can tell you how a lemon differs in taste from a lime or how it feels to chew a grass-fed strip-loin steak versus ground beef, until you do it, it doesn't mean much. I can pack these pages with descriptions about the basics of flavor profiles—salty and sweet, sour and bitter, acidic and basic, nutty and herbal, umami—but until you put those in your mouth and experience them, it ain't gonna help you much.

So, ultimately, I decided to fill the pages of this book—and your plates—with recipes that have been tested rigorously and enjoyed with gluttony, and let you take it from there.

Contrary to your mother's advice, I suggest you pick up and put everything you can in your mouth. And then invite me to dinner.

The Boozy Larder (a.k.a. my belly)

What you do in the pantry of your own home and with whom is none of my business. What you stock in there, however, is.

I use the term *pantry* loosely. I know most of us don't have a full walk-in or deep freeze. But we do have a cupboard or two and a fridge. For instance, my wine and canning cellar is the back of my bedroom closet because it's the darkest, coolest, and most even-temperature place in my house. And by house, I mean a 600-square-foot apartment in the middle of Vancouver. Space is tight.

Keeping a well-stocked larder is key to creating the recipes here and

Essential Ingredients

FRESH PRODUCE

- Arugula
- Avocados
- Carrots
- Celery
- Grapefruit
- Lemons
- Limes
- Oranges
- Red onion
- Yellow onion
- Shallots

CHEESE

- Aged Cheddar
- Blue
- Brie
- Cotija or feta
- Cream cheese
- Gruyère
- Mozzarella (fresh) or burrata
- Parmesan (block & fresh, not pre-grated)
- Ricotta

DAIRY

- Full-fat cream
- Organic, pasture-raised eggs
- Plain full-fat Greek yogurt
- Sour cream
- Unsalted butter

NUTS, LEGUMES, AND BEANS

- Almonds
- Black beans
- Brown and green dried lentils
- Hazelnuts
- Lentils
- Peas (frozen)
- Pecans
- Pine nuts
- Walnuts
- White beans (dried and/or canned)

GRAINS AND PASTA

- Corn tortillas
- Finely ground cornmeal
- Macaroni
- Pappardelle
- Pearl barley
- Penne
- Popcorn
- Tagliatelle

PANTRY ITEMS

- Bread crumbs
- Chipotle peppers in adobo sauce
- Coconut milk
- Coffee beans
- Extra-virgin and/or virgin olive oil (good quality)
- Vegetable oil
- Pumpkin purée
- Pure maple syrup
- San Marzano tomatoes
- Tomato paste
- Apple cider vinegar
- Balsamic vinegar (good quality)
- Red and white wine vinegar
- Wildflower honey

CURED AND PRESERVED

- Anchovies
- Black Moroccan olives
- Capers
- Preserved lemons
- Sun-dried tomatoes
- Thick-cut bacon or pancetta

SPICES AND HERBS

- Allspice
- Basil
- Bay leaves
- Cardamom
- Celery seeds
- Chili powder
- Chives
- Cilantro
- Cinnamon (ground and sticks)
- Cloves
- Coriander seeds
- Cumin (seeds and powder)
- Curry powder (yellow and red)
- Dill
- Flat-leaf parsley
- Ginger
- Italian seasoning
- Mustard
- Nutmeg (whole)
- Pepper (black and white)
- Pumpkin pie spice
- Red pepper flakes
- Rosemary
- Salt (coarse, flaky, and smoked unicorn salt—seriously)

- Smoked paprika
- Thyme
- Vanilla beans

BAKING

- Active dry yeast
- All-purpose flour (unbleached)
- Baking powder
- Baking soda
- Cocoa powder (unsweetened)
- Confectioners' sugar
- Cornstarch
- Granulated sugar
- Pure vanilla extract
- Semisweet or dark chocolate

SPIRITS

- Baileys Irish Cream
- Brandy
- Campari
- Chambord
- Cointreau
- Gin
  - classic and clean
  - floral and botanical
- Kalhúa
- Limoncello
- Mezcal
- Rum
  - dark
  - spiced
  - white
- Sherry (dry)
- St-Germain
- Tequila
  - silver
  - reposado
- Whiskey
  - Bourbon
  - Irish
  - Rye

BEER

- Ale
- IPA
- Lager
- Porter
- Stout

WINE

- Port
- Red
- Rosé
- Sparkling
- White

BAR ESSENTIALS

- Apple cider
- Bitters
- Ginger beer
- Ice (crushed, cubed, and big cubes)
- Soda or sparkling water
- Tonic

cooking up success in your kitchen. Because I'm low on space, I'm selective about the number of items I keep on hand. But each and every one is packed with flavor, so if I'm making a recipe I've been drooling over for months or creating a weeknight meal on the fly, I have 175 square feet of delicious options to toss in the pan. I'm not saying it isn't more crowded in my cupboards than an airport at Christmas (because it most definitely is), but I make do.

Of course, this list isn't inclusive of everything you'll find in the book and on any given day—depending on what's at the market—I'll have any variety of other ingredients lurking in the crisper, but these are my essentials and I hope you'll make (at least some of them) yours.

And yes. I keep a lot of cheese. Don't judge me.

Booty

I have a strange urge to shake mine right now. Do it with me! Shake it like a Polaroid picture! Yeah!

Okay, now that's out of the way.

I can't stand—nay, loathe with a spite that would knock that glass clean out of your hand and smote you on the spot—unnecessary gadgets and toys.

At least in the kitchen.

I'm a firm believer that when our spaces are crowded, so is our mind. I like everything to have a place and for it to be put there. Just ask my fiancé—my need to continually tidy drives him mad. So, when someone gifts me a superfluous tool that just takes up more of the limited drawer space I have, I cringe. And try to channel "the force" to slap the giver with it.

The last thing I want to do is tell you that you need a bunch of expensive shit in your cabinets. So, I won't. But I will give you a brief list of the tools, the loot and the booty that will make your life easier in the kitchen and make it possible for you to dish up every recipe in this book.

BBQ OR INDOOR GRILL
I like to grill. Nothing smells better to me than something on the BBQ. But if you don't have a BBQ, or can't have a BBQ, an indoor electric grill will suffice.

BENCH SCRAPER

I use this bad boy for multiple tasks: prying sticky flour from the counter, applying frosting to cakes, herding peppercorns that escape as I'm trying to refill the peppermill.

BOTTLE OPENER

Um, duh. A bartender's wine crank (the small handheld one that could fit in your back pocket or purse) will open wine and beer bottles alike.

BOWLS

I have a sizable collection of bowls. It's a problem, really.

All you really need though are three mixing bowls of various sizes (small, medium, large) and a few oven-safe ramekins.

I use my stainless-steel mixing bowls almost every day, while I keep one glass bowl on reserve that sits nicely on the top of my medium pot to function as a double boiler for melting chocolate or . . . yep. Generally for melting chocolate.

Note: When I specify a nonreactive bowl or other container, reach for stainless steel or glass.

CAN OPENER

I don't buy a lot of processed or canned ingredients, but some of the few things I do rely on are San Marzano tomatoes, canned beans, and chipotle peppers in adobo sauce. Getting a can opener that fits well in your hand is a must.

CHERRY PITTER

If you like your bourbon-soaked cherries as much as I do (and I know you do), one of these is instrumental so you don't break your teeth on a cherry pit after you pour your fifth finger of bourbon for the evening.

CITRUS SQUEEZER/JUICER

The secret ingredient in most of my dishes—which I suppose is not so secret anymore—is citrus. Just as with onions and garlic, most of my dishes have some kind of fruity, acidic element. It's something that can take a dish from "meh" to "MINE!"

You can buy traditional citrus juicers that grind the fruit over the top of the phallic, ridged protrusion or you can get hand juicers where the fruit sits inside the mechanism and a gear pushes the juice out with the force of your press.

Either way, you'll get way more juice for your squeeze with one of these than without one.

COCKTAIL SHAKER

Again, duh.

I recommend the Boston shaker, which takes a bit of finesse to hold the two ends together when you shake, but it's much easier than trying to pry the top off the cheaper metal ones that tend to stick together when they get frosty.

You can also use a mason jar to shake drinks, but be careful—you don't want to shatter it by a forceful muddle or smashing the ice into the end of it with an overzealous shake.

COCKTAIL STIRRING SPOON

This long, twisty spoon allows you to mix cocktails in a way that delicately chills a drink but doesn't bash the ice all to hell. You could use a regular spoon, but why would you when these are so cool?

They're also good for bashing ice cubes into crushed ice or layering drinks, if you're into that kind of thing.

COOLING RACKS

Cooling racks are essential for letting meat rest, baking cool, and bacon drain. By placing food on these, rather than directly on the cutting board, counter, or paper towels, you let air circulate, which in these three cases result in a juicier steak, fluffier cake, and crispier 'con.

CUTTING BOARDS

As with bowls, I have a cutting board surplus. Generally three boards will getcha off—a small one for cocktail garnishes, a medium one for average cooking, and a large one for when you need to prep a lot of stuff.

It's also great to have a nice wooden or marble one for serving salads or cheese on.

FOOD PROCESSOR

I would die without my food processor. Okay, I probably wouldn't die but I certainly wouldn't have such silky sauces, tender soups, or crunchy crusts. I use mine so often it sits on the counter right beside the toaster.

You can also use a blender.

FRUIT CORER

This isn't something that's absolutely vital to your kitchen, but it helps preserve the shape of fruit by removing the core without chopping the ingredient. I use mine regularly for wine-poached pears as well as home-made apple chips.

GLASSWARE

Unless you're looking to start your own restaurant and bar (or you have a glassware fetish as I do), you don't need every glass under the sun to serve drinks. A few simple glasses can generally do the job and look good doin' it.

For beer and very juicy drinks with ice: tall, thinner glasses or mason jars.

For more booze-forward cocktails: rocks or old-fashioned glasses are key and very versatile for drinks with less juice. I even use them for margaritas and sours.

For martinis or cocktails without ice in the finished drink: coupe glasses. They just feel nice.

For wine: a standard, high-quality, thin-rimmed red wineglass can be used for red, white, and rosé, while flutes really are optimal for sparkling wine. Stems—like pants—are optional.

ICE-CREAM MAKER OR ATTACHMENT

Before I got mine I was like, "Whoa, I'm never making my own ice cream."

Now that I have one I'm like, "Whoa, I need to make my own ice cream."

Mine is an attachment for my KitchenAid stand mixer and I love it.

MANDOLINE SLICER

Unless your knife skills are quick as a cat and consistently regular like a bowl of bran flakes, a mandoline slicer will make your life 90 percent easier. It juliennes, it slices, it dices, and it does it superfast. You can get a decent one—my favorite, from OXO, has multiple thickness settings and stores well—for less than $40.

MASON JARS (WITH LIDS)

I use these for everything. Aside from canning: mixing salad dressings, shaking cocktails, storing *dulce de leche*, keeping dried spices, presenting elements on cheese boards, displaying flowers, glassware, and the list goes on. As I said, I use them for everything.

Lids are only good for canning once, because after you've used the seal, there's a risk of inadequate sealing a second time. Instead of throwing them away, I mark the top of them with a black felt-tip pen and keep them around for the other uses already mentioned.

MEASURING CUPS & SPOONS

For cooking, most of my measurements are approximate and I encourage you to adjust them according to taste. Rarely does a quarter-cup of onions or an extra tablespoon of booze really affect the success of a finished dish; it's flexible.

For baking, though, I'm no master baker. So, I measure the hell out of everything every single time.

I have one 4-cup measuring cup, a set of nested measuring cups that range from ¼ cup to 1 cup, and a set of measuring spoons. For someone who bakes only a few times a year or so, that's enough.

MEAT THERMOMETER

I don't use a meat thermometer. I've cooked meat enough times that I have a feel for it and I generally know when a steak is done simply by touching it. But until you feel comfortable eyeballing chicken or a roast, a meat thermometer comes in quite handy.

MICROPLANES

The best invention. Probably ever. I keep three Microplane products within arm's reach and use all three regularly: a fine-holed one for grating citrus, garlic, nutmeg, and other spices; a medium-holed one for shaving Parmesan and chocolate; and a large-holed one (a.k.a. my cheese grater) for shredding vegetables, bigger cheese jobs, and the like.

MUDDLER

A muddler comes in handy when extracting oils and flavors from herbs or crushing sugar in a drink. You could use a wooden spoon, but the teeth on the end of the muddler help to do this delicately, without pulverizing everything in the mixing glass.

Wood ones are fine and beautiful but metal or plastic ones will last much longer.

PARCHMENT PAPER

The day I discovered parchment paper, my life changed for the better. It keeps baked goods from sticking to pans and breaded food from getting soggy on the cutting board, and wraps up halibut in a neat little parcel and steams it to delicious and savory awesomeness.

During the creation of this book I've discovered white parchment tends to be thinner and tears more easily, whereas darker parchment seems to be stronger. I like having both because I'm greedy like Wall Street.

POTS

As a recipe developer and food blogger, I'm embarrassed to say how old most of my pots and pans are; my parents got them before I was born. At the time this book comes out, I'll be thirty-six. They've lasted the test of time with the exception of one that met her maker about a year ago. Fortunately, there was no boiling water in the pot when the handle shattered.

For our purposes, three heavy-bottomed, nonwarped, stainless-steel pots should do you—one small, one medium, and one large.

I also have a Le Creuset stockpot that I use for soups and stews and do most of my small-batch canning in.

Finally, a slow cooker is vital for those days you don't want to turn on the oven but want a party platter of Cuervo & Tecate Pork Carnitas (page 100) or a nice hot piping bowl of Mom's Stout Baked Beans (page 164).

PANS

For stovetop cooking, I suggest you invest in a 12- to 14-inch cast-iron frying pan (be careful with these on glass cooktops!), a large non-stick frying pan, and a wok.

Cast iron creates a sear on food like nothing else and has even heat across the base (plus it can go in the oven). A large, nonstick frying pan works well for cooking such things as risotto, poaching asparagus, or simmering meat, such as Lager Simmered Chicken Thighs (page 121) or even Rob Roy Braised Short Ribs (page 122). A deep wok doubles as a quick cooker of vegetables and a deep fryer!

For oven cooking, you can rely on a couple of shallow rimmed baking sheets (I even cook my Margherita "Margarita" Pizza [page 155] on these) and a couple of 2-inch-deep roasting pans.

When it comes to baking, much of what's listed here will do. But I enjoy also having a couple of small Bundt pans for adorable Apple Cider Pound Cakes (page 179) and a 9-inch-square baking dish for such things as Raspberry Vodka Brownies & Grenach (page 203) or Classic Polenta (page 230).

And if you're into Classic NY-Style Margarita Cheesecake (page 188) or pretty cakes on cake platters, such as my Layered Naked

Champagne Cake (page 208), springform pans are your new best friend. These allow the sides and bottom of the pan to be removed for fanciful presentation.

ROLLING PIN

I use this to beat my fiancé when he doesn't bring home flowers. JK, JK.

But I do use one to bash spices, crush ice, and roll pizza dough. It's quite handy.

SHOT GLASS OR JIGGER

Unless you want to eyeball your drinks, a single-shot glass or jigger will ensure the measurements and flavors are balanced in your cocktails.

SILICONE BRUSHES

These are indispensable for applying such things as BBQ sauce on burgers, egg wash on phyllo pastry, and olive oil on crostini. I love them.

SPATULAS

For flipping, stirring, and spanking.

STABBY THINGS

You don't need a lot of knives in your kitchen. A good, sharp chef's knife can do just about anything, including chopping, dicing, julienning, crushing, mincing, and even slicing bread.

Beyond that, a paring knife is useful for doing smaller jobs, such as coring an apple or removing the skin off a knob of ginger, and a filleting knife is great if you work with fish a ton.

Finally, steak knives are good for steak. Obvi.

An aside: If you spend good money on a chef's knife, you should really maintain it. Don't let it soak in water; instead, dry and put it away when you're done with it, and sharpen it regularly. You can get a steel to sharpen them (Gordon Ramsay has an excellent tutorial on YouTube on how to do this without gutting yourself) or take them to a knife shop. *Please* don't use those little handheld machines that shear off part of your blade. That's the quickest way to ruin your beautiful, expensive knife.

STAND MIXER

You can generally do anything with an electric hand mixer, whisk, or your bare hands that you can do with a stand mixer. A stand mixer simply makes it all the simpler. And less manual. Which frees up your hands to pour yourself a cocktail.

STRAINERS

Having a variety of strainers is awesome. I keep a large, wide-bowl strainer for soups and boiled vegetables; a fine-mesh one for creating silky sauces, clear shrubs, and draining cheese; and an even smaller, cone-shaped one (think: like a tea strainer) for straining cocktails.

Beyond that, you may want to get either a Hawthorne strainer or julep strainer for your drinks if you want to be accurate. And awesome.

TINFOIL

I mainly use tinfoil as a tent for meat that's resting, but it's also good in a pinch if you don't have a lid for a pot or pan.

It's also key for blocking alien radio signals.

TONGS

For flipping on the grill, lifting jars out of a water bath, and saving your fingers from getting messy while handling raw meat.

WHISKS

I keep two: one smaller French-style whisk for sauces and one larger, balloon-style one for whisking air into eggs and pretending it's a microphone.

WOODEN SPOONS, LADLES, & SERVING SPOONS

There's something soothing about stirring tomato sauce with a wooden spoon or dipping a ladle into a big pot of soup—something homey. But more than that, these kinds of spoons are great for getting into the far corners of a pot of sauce, scraping up bits of melted, crispy cheese from a pan, or simply dishing up.

And isn't that what we all aim to do when we sit down to a meal?
Let's do that.

I generally start and end a great meal with a good, stiff drink.

It didn't start that way though. My first memorable experience with alcohol involved two Wildberry Coolers and a very dark basement on a farm in rural Alberta. Yeah, I was hard-core. For sure.

It wasn't until I got my first job serving in a bar that I began to understand—or at least was able tell the difference between—beer and wine.

There were a few occasions before this job that I'd gotten to know alcohol—clearly some moments when she and I got a little too friendly, if you know what I mean—but this job was the gateway. The looking glass, if you will.

Little did I know I was going to fall into a pile of other glasses: highball, martini, collins, old-fashioned, coupe, margarita, snifter, pint, Nick & Nora, fizz, julep, stein, red wine, white wine, stemless, and champagne.

Nor did I realize the complexity, thoughtfulness, and intricacies involved in creating a libation worth drinking.

Like cooking, mixing drinks takes some basic knowledge and a bit of practice to achieve the perfect cocktail. I've included what you need to know to make the drinks in this book, but there's certainly more to learn. I hope this will inspire you to a lifetime of good drinking.

But for now, refer to my brilliance and start here. Clearly I'm nothing if not humble.

cocktails

Boulevardier   35

"Moscow" Dark & Stormy   36

French 75 (2.0 Edition)   39

Classic Lime Daiquiri   40

Mint Cucumber & Smoky
Jalapeño Margarita   43

Elderflower Summer Spritz   44

Dirty Sexy Coffee Drinks (a.k.a. Shafts)   47

Rhuby-Tom (Rhubarb Tom Collins)   48

Maple Bacon Bourbon Manhattan with
Bacon Salt   51

Snackin' Caesar   52

Boozy Beet Shrub   55

Cinnamon Apple Whiskey Sour   56

Boulevardier

A cousin to the Negroni (gin, sweet vermouth, and Campari), the Boulevardier was originally created by Erskine Gwynne, in the 1920s. It's something even non-bourbon drinkers can enjoy. And if I can bring more bourbon to the masses, I'll cheers to that.

INSTRUCTIONS

1. Pour the bourbon whiskey, Campari, and sweet vermouth into a cocktail shaker or mason jar.

2. Top with ice.

3. Stir with a cocktail stirrer for 60 seconds.

4. Strain into a coupe glass.

5. Garnish with an orange twist and, if desired, Bourbon-Soaked Cherries. Enjoy!

Serves: 1

INGREDIENTS

1½ ounces bourbon whiskey

1 ounce Campari

1 ounce sweet vermouth

Ice

To garnish: orange twist

Optional garnish: Bourbon-Soaked Cherries (page 216)

Tipsy Tip

We stir this cocktail—not shake it—because we want to chill the beverage but not overly dilute the flavors or muddy the clarity. Stirring maintains the silky feel of the drink without aerating it (shaking causes this). The general rule: Booze-forward drinks should be stirred, whereas drinks with juice should be shaken.

"Moscow" Dark & Stormy

Serves: 1

INGREDIENTS

3 ounces dark rum

1 cup (hard or regular) ginger beer

Juice of 2 limes

Ice

To garnish: lime wheels

Optional garnish: a little sea salt

Tipsy Tip

Serve these in classic Moscow Mule copper mugs and alongside the Dark and Stormy Kettle Corn for a themed evening of rum, ginger beer, and lime!

This drink evolved out of the Dark and Stormy Kettle Corn (page 183). It was a fortuitous aftereffect. A "happy accident," if you will. This is the love child of a Moscow Mule (vodka, a spicy ginger beer, and lime juice) and a Dark and Stormy (dark rum and ginger beer)—arguably two of the most refreshing cocktails of all time. A blend of flavors that is perfect for spring when the weather is still tumultuous and you're ready for a little sunshine.

INSTRUCTIONS

1. Pour the rum, ginger beer, and lime juice into your preferred cocktail glass.

2. Top with lots of ice and stir for about 25 seconds.

3. Garnish with a lime wheel. If using the salt, lightly dip one corner of the lime into the salt. Position the lime with the salt facing outside the cocktail. Drink.

French 75 (2.0 Edition)

There are literally hundreds of cocktails involving champagne, some of the most popular being the Kir Royale (crème de cassis topped with champagne), the champagne cocktail (a bitters-soaked sugar cube topped with champagne), the mimosa (orange juice topped with champagne), and the French 75—gin, champagne, and lemon.

Building on the classic French 75, I've added a shot of limoncello to really brighten the thing up. And make it boozier. Obvi. This is the French 75 (2.0 Edition). And it's ridiculously refreshing.

INSTRUCTIONS

1. Pour the limoncello and gin into a champagne flute.

2. Top with the wine.

3. Garnish with a sprig of fresh thyme. Enjoy!

Serves: 1

INGREDIENTS

1½ ounces limoncello

1½ ounces gin

4 ounces dry sparkling wine

Thyme sprigs

Tipsy Tip

To get wild and crazy, make your own limoncello; it'll be the best you've ever had! Simply buy the cleanest, highest-proof 750 ml bottle of vodka you can find and 12 organic lemons—regular or Meyer. Zest the lemons (but not the bitter white pith underneath) and place the zest in a large mason jar. Top with vodka. Store in a dark, cool place for 2 to 6 weeks. Strain. Sweeten with up to 2 cups of Simple Syrup (page 218), to taste. Chill. Limoncello will keep for up to 1 month in the fridge or up to 12 in the freezer. Use in such cocktails as this one, the Limoncello Shrimp with Black Pepper & Mango Salsa (page 64) or simply sip after dinner. Note: The longer you let the limoncello sit, the mellower and more flavorful it will become.

Classic Lime Daiquiri

Serves: 1

INGREDIENTS

A little sugar or coarse sea salt, depending on your preference

Lime wedges

3 ounces good-quality light rum

1½ ounces Simple Syrup (page 218)

Juice of 2–3 limes, depending on your preference

Ice

To garnish: lime wheels, sliced chile pepper, or fresh berries

Tipsy Tip

It's especially important that you use fresh lime juice in this recipe. I usually squeeze a pint-size mason jar's worth of juice in one go, so I'm set for the evening. This will make about six daiquiris and requires 15 to 18 limes, depending on how juicy they are. To extract more liquid from citrus, roll it on its side for 10 seconds to help release the juice!

This is one of the easiest, simplest cocktails you can make. And if you have enough of them, you might just write the next great American novel. Okay, maybe not. But Ernest Hemingway—despite all his crazy—did write some pretty damn successful stories. He also drank daiquiris like the world was running out of rum.

As with desserts, I'm not a big sweet-flavor fan when it comes to cocktails. But a well-balanced daiquiri has a special place in my heart. Maybe it's the inner novelist in me.

INSTRUCTIONS

1. Prepare the Simple Syrup; set aside to cool completely before using.

2. Pour the sugar or salt into a shallow dish.

3. Run a lime wedge over the rim of a rocks glass and then dip the glass into the sugar or salt, twisting your wrist to ensure even coverage. Gently shake off any excess. Set aside.

4. Pour the rum, simple syrup, and lime juice into a cocktail shaker or mason jar.

5. Top with ice.

6. Cover and shake for 30 seconds.

7. Pour into the prepared glass.

8. Garnish with a fresh lime wheel and one or two slices of chile pepper, depending on how spicy you like it. Alternatively, you can garnish with fresh berries for a sweeter version.

Mint Cucumber & Smoky Jalapeño Margarita

Bourbon will always be my first love. Nay, my true love. But a good-quality tequila is a lot like that hot summer fling you had when you were full of youth—sexy, dirty, and all kinds of wrong in the best kinds of ways. This recipe was the last one that made it into the book; it wasn't supposed to be here. But I was so blown away by the flavors of the drink that I just had to share it with you. These margaritas are smoky. Salty. Totally crisp. And there's tequila. Lots and lots of tequila.

A tip: Don't skimp on the garnish—the margarita-soaked cucumber slices are kind of the secret ingredient.

INSTRUCTIONS

1. First, grill the jalapeño: Preheat your grill or broiler to 450°F. Place the jalapeño on the grate and blacken thoroughly, 2 to 3 minutes per side. Remove from the heat and let cool to the touch. Chop roughly.

2. As the pepper chars, make the salt rim. Combine the salt and smoked paprika in a shallow rimmed dish. Set aside.

3. Prepare your serving glass: Take one of the lime wedges and run it along the lip of the glass. Dip into the salt mixture and twist your wrist to coat the rim. Gently shake off any excess. Set aside.

4. Now for the good stuff: Make your cocktail! Place the blackened jalapeño, cucumber, sugar, and Cointreau in a large mason jar or cocktail shaker. Muddle with a bit of force until the sugar breaks down.

5. Add the mint leaves, tequila, and lime juice. Muddle lightly. You don't want to destroy the mint, but to extract the oils.

6. Top with ice, cover tightly, and shake until your arm hurts.

7. Place a small, fine-mesh strainer over the prepared glass and pour the liquid through it.

8. Garnish with a lime wheel and slice of cucumber. Bottoms up!

Serves: 1

INGREDIENTS

½ jalapeño pepper

½ cup flaky, coarse sea salt (e.g., Maldon)

1 teaspoon smoked paprika

Fresh lime wedges

⅓ cup diced cucumber

1 cube brown or cane sugar

1½ ounces Cointreau

1 tablespoon lightly packed fresh mint leaves

3 ounces reposado or silver tequila (or mezcal, if you're feeling adventurous)

⅓ cup fresh lime juice (approximately 5 limes)

Ice

To garnish: lime wheels and slices of cucumber

Tipsy Tip

Oh, for the love of tequila. For the purposes of this margarita, look for 100 percent agave reposado or blanco (a.k.a. silver) tequila. I love George Clooney's Casamigos Reposado because, well, George Clooney. But it also has this incredible caramel aroma and full mouthfeel. It's also a little gritty at the end. Which is how I like my tequila. And my summer flings.

Elderflower Summer Spritz

Serves: 1

INGREDIENTS

1½ ounces St-Germain
   liqueur

1½ ounces vodka

4 ounces good-quality tonic
   water

Ice

To garnish: long, thin slices
   of cucumber and lemon
   twists

Tipsy Tip

To make a big batch for a
party, multiply the number of
alcohol shots by person, dice
the cucumber into cubes, and
chuck it all in a large pitcher.
Top with the required amount
of tonic water and ice. Stir.

This cocktail is like getting punched in the face by summer. In a good
way. It evolved out of the need to help my mom use up some of the alcohol she purchased while testing recipes for this book. So, I made her
a cocktail. This is a recipe that's well suited to summer BBQs or community happy hours, which is how she imbibes hers. Here's to moms
everywhere. And the daughters that love them.

INSTRUCTIONS

1. Pour the St-Germain liqueur and vodka into a cocktail shaker or
   mason jar.

2. Top with ice.

3. Cover and shake vigorously for 30 seconds.

4. Pour everything into a tall glass and top with the tonic.

5. Garnish with cucumber and a lemon twist. Enjoy!

Dirty Sexy Coffee Drinks (a.k.a. Shafts)

I first discovered the Shaft during my serving days on Vancouver Island. Preshift, we'd chug this concoction through a straw to get us through those long nights of waiting tables. Once I left the industry, my friends and I continued the tradition before any big night out. You know, to get us through those long nights of sitting at tables. And now it gives me an excuse to restock my bar with Baileys, Kahlúa, and vodka. No complaints here.

Strong coffee, creamy Baileys, sweet Kahlúa, and a healthy dose of vodka—these things go together like ramma lamma lamma ka dinga da dinga dong!

INSTRUCTIONS

1. Fill two glasses with ice cubes.

2. Measure the alcohol into a shaker or large mason jar. Top with the coffee and then ice cubes. Cover tightly, shake vigorously for 20 seconds.

3. Pour into the prepared glasses and top with a little heavy cream, if desired.

4. Throw a straw in each one and suck that baby back as fast as you can.

Serves: 2

INGREDIENTS

3 ounces vodka

1½ ounces Kahlúa

1½ ounces Baileys Irish Cream

2 cups very strong brewed coffee, or ½ cup brewed espresso, fully chilled

Ice cubes

Optional: splash of heavy cream to top

Tipsy Tip

If you'd rather savor than shoot these bad boys, make a double batch of coffee and freeze half of it in ice cube trays. Then use those instead of regular ice in the drink. As you sip, you'll maintain the caffeinated flavor of the drink and won't water it down.

Rhuby-Tom (Rhubarb Tom Collins)

Serves: 1

INGREDIENTS

1 fresh rhubarb stalk, chopped into 1-inch pieces

1 cube brown sugar

½ teaspoon ground cardamom

Juice of 1 tangelo or other "sweet" orange

Freshly ground black pepper

3 ounces of your favorite gin

Ice

1 cup good-quality tonic water

To garnish: a ribbon of tangelo zest

The best thing about spring is the abundance of fresh rhubarb. And gin. Okay, gin is always in abundance—at least in my house. Thank goodness. But rhubarb isn't, so I get my fill while I can. This is the Rhuby-Tom. A seasonal drink that's delightfully tart, slightly sweet, and just the right amount of rosy. Pair with a plate of fresh Limoncello Shrimp (page 64) or a heaping pile of Mezcal Pan Asparagus (page 159) or JD Mac & Peas (page 153). Or all of the above.

INSTRUCTIONS

1. Place the rhubarb, brown sugar, cardamom, orange juice, and pepper in a shaker or mason jar.

2. Muddle until well pummeled.

3. Add the gin and fill with ice.

4. Cover and shake with vigor until your arm aches a little.

5. Strain into a glass and top with ice.

6. Cap it all off with a little tonic and garnish with a ribbon of tangelo zest.

Tipsy Tip

A lot of small-batch gins have some pretty complex flavors that I love, especially Phillips Coastal Forest Stump Gin or Defender Island Smoked Rosemary Gin—two of my favorites. Because of the delicate flavor of the rhubarb though, look for a more traditional gin for this drink, such as Hendrick's or another local distiller's that's cleaner.

Maple Bacon Bourbon Manhattan with Bacon Salt

I just couldn't help myself: Bourbon. And maple. And bacon.

Serves: 1

PREPARE THE BACON SALT

1. Place a large frying pan over medium heat. Cook the bacon in batches until crispy, draining on paper towels as they come out of the pan. Alternatively, if you prefer to cook bacon in the oven, you can. Just make sure it gets good and crispy!

2. Place the bacon in a food processor with the coarse sea salt. Process at high speed until the bacon is finely ground with the salt.

PREPARE THE COCKTAIL

1. Rub the orange wedge around the rim of a rocks glass to wet the lip. Dip into the bacon salt, gently shaking off any excess. Set aside.

2. Place the bourbon whiskey, vermouth, maple syrup, and bitters in a cocktail shaker or large mason jar. Top with crushed ice and stir for 45 seconds.

3. Strain into the prepared glass and garnish with any (or all) of the suggested garnishes.

Note

If using the Bacon Salt right away, pour into a shallow bowl. If saving for later, transfer to a clean, airtight container. The bacon salt will keep in the fridge for up to 2 weeks.

BACON SALT

One 12-ounce package thick-cut bacon

1 cup coarse sea salt

COCKTAIL

1 orange wedge

3 ounces good-quality bourbon whiskey

1 ounce sweet vermouth

½ ounce pure maple syrup

Dash of Angostura (or preferred) bitters

Crushed ice

To garnish: orange twist, boozy cherries, a little bacon salt, and/or a slice of cooked bacon

Tipsy Tip

This recipe creates more Bacon Salt than you're likely to use on your cocktail. Use it on EVERYTHING. Grilled meats, roasted vegetables, Snackin' Caesar rims (page 52), and sprinkled on breakfast cereal. Okay, don't do that last one. But try the rest!

Snackin' Caesar

Serves: 1

CELERY SALT

½ cup celery seeds

⅓ cup Maldon salt

1 tablespoon freshly ground white pepper

COCKTAIL

1 lime slice

3 ounces gin

1½ teaspoons sriracha hot sauce

Splash of pickle juice

2 shakes Worcestershire sauce

½ tablespoon grated fresh horseradish

Ice cubes

¾ cup Mott's Clamato juice

To garnish: lime wedges

Optional garnish: pickled bean, celery stalk, cube of cheese, pickles, pepperoni stick, cooked chicken wing, pickled pepper, cooked clam on toast.

Tipsy Tip

If you're unable to find Clamato where you are, feel free to substitute tomato juice. It's thicker and not quite as salty, but you'll get the overall experience.

This bad boy is an amped-up classic that hails from Canada. With gin and pickle juice. A classic Caesar is served at brunch or lunch on the weekends, often patio-side. It's a "hair of the dog" kind of thing, though I regularly reach for one when it's too early for a beer. Or it's Sunday. Or Wednesday. While it's traditionally made with vodka, I'm more a gin kinda gal. So, I ran with it. The result? A drink that is well balanced and not overly spicy, and, when garnished with so many delicious treats, brunch in a glass!

PREPARE THE CELERY SALT

1. Place all the ingredients in a mortar and pestle. Bash until well combined and the seeds are fragrant and have started to break down.

PREPARE THE COCKTAIL

1. Gently wet the lip of a wide-mouth mason jar or tall glass with a slice of lime. Dip the glass in the celery salt and turn in a couple of circles to ensure even coating. Shake off any excess.

2. Combine the gin, sriracha, pickle juice, Worcestershire sauce, and horseradish in the glass. Gently stir the mixture with a cocktail spoon.

3. Top with ice. Add the Clamato juice.

4. Garnish with a lime wedge with a slit to hold it on the edge of the glass, and any other garnish your imagination can concoct!

Note

If using the Celery Salt right away, pour into a shallow bowl. If saving for later (or gifting!), pour into a clean jar with a tight-fitting lid and store in the cupboard for up to 6 months.

Boozy Beet Shrub

I have Jayme Marie Henderson, Emily Han, and Mike Dietsch to thank for introducing me to the juicy beasts that are shrubs. At this time of year, I constantly have at least a few jars macerating in the back of the fridge. This smoky beet shrub is an earthy cocktail and a refreshing way to cool down after a fruitful morning at the farmers' market. In fact, you can score just about every single ingredient directly from the farmers themselves. Now, that's a delicious haul!

PREPARE THE SHRUB

1. Place the vinegar, sugar, mint, and smoked paprika in a nonreactive bowl. Whisk well to combine.

2. Add the beets. Mix well and cover.

3. Place in the fridge to macerate for 2 days, giving the mixture a good stir halfway through.

4. Remove the solids with a fine-mesh strainer and pour the liquid into a clean jar.

PREPARE THE COCKTAIL

1. Pour the lemon juice, beet shrub, and gin into a cocktail shaker or mason jar.

2. Top with ice cubes.

3. Stir to chill for 20 seconds.

4. Fill a rocks glass with crushed ice.

5. Strain the liquid into the prepared glass.

6. Top with tonic water and garnish with a sprig of fresh mint. Enjoy!

Note

The shrub recipe makes 1¼ cups. Store in the fridge, tightly sealed, for 4 to 6 weeks.

Serves: 1

SHRUB

1 cup cider vinegar

1 cup organic cane sugar

⅓ cup fresh mint leaves

2 teaspoons smoked paprika

1 teaspoon coarse sea salt

4 medium beets, diced into ½-inch cubes

COCKTAIL

1 tablespoon lemon juice

1½ ounces beet shrub

3 ounces good-quality gin

Ice cubes

Crushed ice

Good-quality tonic water

To garnish: sprig of fresh mint

Tipsy Tip

Once the shrub has been strained, reserve the beet solids for munching. They're all pickley and would be delicious on a Cheese Plate (page 211)!

Cinnamon Apple Whiskey Sour

Serves: 1

INGREDIENTS

2 tablespoons ground cinnamon

2 tablespoons sugar

½ apple, cored and thinly sliced

3 ounces bourbon whiskey (Maker's Mark or Woodford Reserve should do ya)

1½ ounces Simple Syrup (page 218)

Dash of Angostura bitters

Juice of 1 lemon

Ice cubes

½ cup decent dry apple cider

To garnish: small sprig of fresh rosemary

I always look forward to the things that fall brings—cooler evenings, hoodies, crunchy leaves, and drinking red wine again. Plus, you know, apples. There's a familiarity about them—like coming home after a long trip away. Or finding yourself in the company of good friends you haven't seen in a while. Or that book whose cover has seen the bathtub two times too many.

This cocktail tempts us with warm spices; woodsy undertones; and lots of sweet, succulent, fresh apples. Tuck into one as the evening allows.

INSTRUCTIONS

1. Prepare the Simple Syrup; set aside to cool completely before using.

2. Place the cinnamon and sugar in a shallow bowl. Mix to combine. Set aside.

3. Run a slice of apple halfway along the rim of a rocks glass.

4. Pour the whiskey, simple syrup, bitters, and lemon juice into a mason jar or shaker. Add a big handful of ice cubes, cover, and shake for 10 seconds.

5. Strain into the prepared glass. Top with the cider.

6. Run the slice of apple through the cinnamon-sugar mixture and drop as a garnish in the drink. Spear with the rosemary sprig.

Tipsy Tip

If you're feeling adventurous (and after a couple of these, why wouldn't you be?), toss a large organic, pasture-raised egg white into the shaker to create a froth that's indicative (and enjoyable!) of a classic sour.

All good things come to those who wait. So they say. I wouldn't know; patience has never been my strong suit.

When it comes to the things I love—crostini, bourbon, itsy-bitsy teeny-weenie yellow polka-dot bikinis, Joseph Gordon-Levitt—I want them. And I want them now. Thank the sweet heavens for amuse-bouches, appetizers, and bar snacks!

Unlike birthday presents, some of the best dishes come in small packages. Big flavors, small plates. A drizzle of something sweet, a sprinkle of flaky sea salt, an extra few minutes in the oven that elevates an ingredient from good to something sultry or effervescent.

Think about fresh-off-the-vine summer tomatoes. Eaten raw they're like sunshine candy. Perfection, right? But drizzle them with some good-quality olive oil and a bit of salt and pepper and chuck 'em in a low-heat oven for an hour and a half and you end up with something that can only be described as an unadulterated, uncensored, sinfully delicious orgasm of flavor.

Never mind the lascivious reaction spawned by fresh shrimp soaked in homemade limoncello (page 64). Or the explosion (of flavor) you'll discover when you pop a Strawberry Chambord Whipped Stilton Cheese Toast in your mouth (page 61).

It's these moments before the main meal that awaken our palate, heighten our senses, tease our belly, and get the liquor flowing.

Bottoms up!

appetizers & bar snacks

Strawberry Chambord Whipped Stilton Cheese Toasts   61

Estrella Jamón Croquettes   62

Limoncello Shrimp with Black Pepper & Mango Salsa   64

Red Wine Chorizo with Blistered Cherry Tomatoes & Fresh Herbs   67

Cheese & Rum Marinated Pineapple Sticks   68

"Fundo" Pull-Apart Bread   71

Brandy-Laced Chicken Liver Pâté   72

Vodka-Spiked Butternut Squash "Parcels" & Bloody Mary Tomato Jam   74

Crunchy Pommes Frites with Madeira Balsamic Reduction   76

Verdejo Habas con Jamón (Fava Beans with Spanish Ham & Wine)   79

Strawberry Chambord Whipped Stilton Cheese Toasts

This recipe is the pinnacle of farm-fresh opulence. Chambord is a black raspberry liqueur that marries softly with fresh summer fruit. Combined with the bold flavor of the "king" of blue cheese, these little crostini are something to be served at any special event—weekend brunch, a wedding shower, or even something as simple as a gathering of friends on a Thursday night.

INSTRUCTIONS

1. Pour the vinegar and Chambord into a small saucepan over medium-high heat. Bring to a light boil. Lower the heat to medium-low and simmer for 15 minutes, or until the mixture thickens, reduces by half, and coats the back of a spoon. Set aside. If it thickens too much as it cools, just add a couple of tablespoons of water and reheat. Note: Watch it once it starts to reduce; it can do so quickly, and if you reduce too far, you'll end up with a hard candy and a ruined pot.

2. Once the syrup cools, remove the tops from the berries, dice the fruit into 1-inch cubes, and toss them in the cooled reduction along with ½ teaspoon of coarse sea salt. Let sit for 10 minutes. Depending on your berries, you may find you have a high liquid content in the bowl after this time; strain most of it out. You don't really want more than ¼ cup of strawberry juice in the bowl.

3. While the berries marinate, set your broiler to low heat and arrange your oven rack to the middle position. Slice the baguette into ½-inch pieces and place on a shallow baking pan. Lightly brush the tops with the oil and season to taste with coarse sea salt and pepper. Place in the oven and toast until golden. Note: Again, watch them—they can quickly go from toasty to burned. I've done that hundreds of times.

4. Place the Stilton crumbles, cream cheese, and ½ teaspoon of coarse sea salt in a bowl. Using a whisk, whip until smooth and airy.

5. Assemble! You can serve this as a platter and let people assemble their own bites or you can finish them off for a fancier presentation: Take a toast and slather a healthy amount of cheese on the base. Lightly press a basil leaf into the cheese and top with a heaping tablespoon of the strawberry mixture, and, if desired, a light sprinkling of Maldon sea salt. Enjoy!

Serves: 6 to 8

INGREDIENTS

½ cup balsamic vinegar

½ cup Chambord (raspberry liqueur)

2 cups farm-fresh strawberries

Coarse sea salt

1 loaf French baguette

1 tablespoon extra-virgin olive oil

Freshly ground black pepper

½ cup blue Stilton, crumbled

⅓ cup cream cheese, softened

½ cup fresh basil leaves

Optional: Maldon sea salt for serving

Tipsy Tip

Blue cheese can have a very strong flavor due to the mold that producers inject or stir into the cheese, but there are varying degrees of the stuff. From mild (Danish Blue, Gorgonzola) to strong (Stilton, Roquefort), experiment to see which your palate prefers.

If you can't bring yourself to eat blue cheese at all (silly, reader), a soft, fresh goat cheese would work here, too.

Estrella Jamón & Croquettes

Yield: About 20 croquettes

INGREDIENTS

5 ⅓ tablespoons unsalted
  butter, at room
  temperature

1 yellow onion, finely
  chopped (1 cup)

2–3 portobello mushrooms,
  finely chopped (2 cups)

2½ cups all-purpose flour

1 cup whole milk

½ cup Estrella (lager-style
  Spanish beer)

¼ cup chicken stock, plus
  extra if needed (page
  224)

½ cup finely chopped *jamón*
  or smoked prosciutto

Freshly ground black pepper

2 large eggs, lightly beaten

1 cup bread crumbs

Canola or vegetable oil for
  deep-frying

Coarse sea salt

To garnish: lemon wedges

It was wandering around the bustling district of La Rambla that I first discovered *jamón* croquettes. I ordered at least three tapas plates, just for myself. No sharesies.

While jamón isn't the cheapest of cured meats, it's worth the extra pennies to experience true Spanish flavors—it took me back. Salty. Crunchy. Velvety. Fatty. Beautiful.

INSTRUCTIONS

1. Melt the butter in a medium-size saucepan over low heat. Add the onion and cook for 5 minutes, or until translucent.

2. Add the mushrooms and cook for 5 minutes, stirring occasionally.

3. Add 2 cups of the flour, and stir over medium-low heat for about a minute, or until the mixture is dry and crumbly and begins to slightly change color. Remove from the heat and add the milk slowly, stirring until smooth.

4. Stir in the beer and chicken stock, and return to the heat. If needed, add a tablespoon or so more liquid to make the mixture smooth. Stir until the mixture comes to a boil and thickens.

5. Stir in the *jamón* and some pepper, then transfer to a mixing bowl and refrigerate for at least 2 hours.

6. Once chilled, put the remaining ½ cup of flour, beaten eggs, and bread crumbs in three separate bowls.

7. Roll heaped spoonfuls of the dough into croquette shapes, 2½ inches long.

8. Toss the croquettes in the flour, then roll in the eggs, and then roll in the bread crumbs.

9. Put on a baking sheet and refrigerate for anywhere between 30 and 45 minutes.

10. Once they are chilled, fill a deep, heavy-based saucepan (or a wok) one-third full of oil and heat over medium-high heat until a cube of bread dropped into the oil browns in 20 seconds. Be sure to have baking soda and/or a fire extinguisher nearby in case you inadvertently set the house on fire!

11. Add the croquettes in batches, being mindful not to splatter or splash the oil at yourself (it's very hot!), and deep-fry for about 3 minutes, carefully turning, until browned.

12. Drain well on paper towels and sprinkle generously with salt. Serve with lemon wedges.

Tipsy Tip

Jamón serrano is a dry-cured ham made from white pigs in Spain, with Iberian pigs being the most prized. The mountain ham is rigorously monitored, then certified with the seal of Consorcio del Jamón Serrano, guarantee-ing that the curing process lasted at least nine months. If you can't find *jamón* at your butcher, you could substitute a smoked prosciutto.

Limoncello Shrimp with Black Pepper & Mango Salsa

Serves: 4

INGREDIENTS

1 tablespoon unsalted butter

1 garlic clove, minced

1 shallot, finely diced

1 cup limoncello

Zest of 1 lemon

1 tablespoon finely chopped flat-leaf parsley

24 large shrimp or spot prawns, deveined and peeled

1 batch Mango Salsa (page 233)

Tipsy Tip

Spot prawns are found in the North Pacific. They are an instant love affair. Sweet. Delicate. If you can get them, use them. Make sure to use wild-caught or sustainably farmed.

There are two ways to make this dish—on the BBQ or in a frying pan on the stovetop. I've included both here, so, regardless of the weather and your preferred method and partiality to sauce (or you want 'em both ways!), you can have your shrimp and eat them, too. I'd be curious to hear which way you like them best.

Make the Mango Salsa first if you are using the stovetop method; if using the BBQ method, make the salsa while the shrimp marinates.

BBQ METHOD

1. Throw all the ingredients, except the shrimp and the Mango Salsa, into a shallow dish and mix well to combine.

2. Skewer the shrimp, six prawns to a stick.

3. Add the shrimp to the mixture and coat well. Let marinate for 30 minutes.

4. Preheat your grill to 450°F.

5. Remove the skewered shrimp from the container, shaking off the excess marinade. Place on the grill and cook, with the lid down, for 2½ to 3 minutes per side, until pink and cooked through.

6. Remove from the heat and serve with crusty bread, a nice salad, and the Mango Salsa.

STOVETOP METHOD

1. Place the butter in a frying pan over medium heat. When it starts to sizzle, add the garlic and shallots. Cook until softened and fragrant, 3 to 4 minutes.

2. Add the shrimp. Sauté for 1½ minutes per side, or until pink.

3. Add the rest of the ingredients and heat through. Simmer for 2 minutes.

4. Remove from the heat, pour the contents of the pan into a large serving dish, and serve with crusty bread, a nice salad, and the Mango Salsa.

Red Wine Chorizo with Blistered Cherry Tomatoes & Fresh Herbs

Is there anything more beautiful in the world than oozy, soft, delicious blistered cherry tomatoes? It's as if the sun was literally slow roasted and then served up family style on a big ole platter. This dish exudes rustic chic—beautiful aromas with a sophisticated flavor profile and a presentation that is dark, rich, and lustrous. Enveloped in a silky red wine sauce that is more than the sum of its parts. It's an experience.

INSTRUCTIONS

1.   Heat the oil in a large frying pan over medium-low heat.

2.   When shimmering (but not smoking), add the onion, season with salt, stir well, and allow to cook for 5 to 7 minutes, stirring occasionally.

3.   When just starting to caramelize, add the garlic and mix well.

4.   When fragrant, throw the chorizo into the pan and brown on all sides. This should take about 5 more minutes.

5.   Pour in the wine, add the tomatoes, a pinch of salt, and the bay leaf, and stir well to combine.

6.   Bring to a simmer and allow the mixture to reduce for about 10 minutes, or until the sauce has thickened and is no longer "soupy."

7.   Discard the bay leaf, add the herbs and butter, and stir to combine.

8.   Serve with a loaf of your favorite bread and, if desired, a few additional herbs sprinkled on top. Eat.

Serves: 4

INGREDIENTS

2 tablespoons olive oil

1 large onion, thinly sliced

Salt

3 garlic cloves, minced

4 links fresh chorizo sausage, sliced into 1-inch pieces

1½ cups dry Spanish red wine

15 cherry tomatoes, halved

1 bay leaf

½ cup chopped fresh herbs (thyme, oregano, and/or flat-leaf parsley)

1 tablespoon unsalted butter

Optional: to serve, crusty bread

Tipsy Tip

If you want to make this into a full meal, serve over rice or with a side of Classic Polenta (230) and more wine. Always more wine.

Cheese & Rum Marinated Pineapple Sticks

Serves: 4

INGREDIENTS

1 pineapple, ends removed and rough outer skin cut away, fruit cut into 1-inch slices

½ cup dark or spiced rum

¼ cup light brown sugar

1 tablespoon olive oil

¼ teaspoon coarse sea salt

FLAVOR VARIATIONS

¼ cup finely chopped fresh mint

1 (7-ounce [200-gram]) container bocconcini mozzarella balls, drained and halved

OR

¼ finely chopped fresh rosemary leaves

10.5 ounces aged Cheddar, cut into 1-inch pieces

Tipsy Tip

The original rendition of this recipe is simply cubed aged Cheddar, drained canned pineapple, and a toothpick. It's not boozy, but it is delicious. If you try it, keep it bite-size and make sure the pineapple sits on top of the cheese on the stick or it'll fall over. But really, still serve it with rum. Maybe a "Moscow" Dark & Stormy (page 36)!

Don't let the simplicity or, ahem, uniqueness of this dish fool you. My Cheese & Rum Marinated Pinapple Sticks are an unpretentious, simple, fast, elegant, and cheap appetizer that is a no-fuss crowd-pleaser. What it lacks in sophistication, it more than makes up for in flavor.

INSTRUCTIONS

1. Place all the ingredients, except the cheese, in a shallow baking dish or large resealable plastic freezer bag. Marinate for 1 to 6 hours.

2. Preheat your grill to medium-high (about 450°F). If it's chucking down outside, you can also use an indoor grill.

3. Shake the excess marinade off the pineapple and grill for 4 to 5 minutes per side, until tender and soft grill marks form.

4. Remove from the heat and let cool slightly to handle.

5. Cut each pineapple wheel into eighths (just like a pie) and skewer right to the end, followed by a wedge of Cheddar or mozzarella ball. Continue until each skewer is full. Enjoy!

"Fundo" Pull-Apart Bread

Warning: This shit is messy.

Second warning: This shit is bananas! I've had one friend say this dish makes her fantasize about a life where she could eat this every night, late at night, and not weigh 1,000 pounds. It'd be a grand life!

Be prepared to eat hot with fondue forks, regular forks, or pitchforks. And have lots of napkins handy.

Serves: 4

INGREDIENTS

1½ cups grated Gruyère

1½ cups grated aged Cheddar

3 tablespoons all-purpose flour

½ teaspoon dry mustard

¼ teaspoon grated nutmeg

1 tablespoon chopped fresh chives

1 round sourdough loaf

4 slices thick-cut bacon, cut into ¼-inch pieces

1 small yellow onion, diced

1 cup lager beer

Dash of Worcestershire sauce

1 garlic clove, minced

5 tablespoons unsalted butter, melted

To garnish: ⅓ cup chopped fresh parsley

INSTRUCTIONS

1. Preheat your oven to 400°F and line a rimmed baking sheet with tinfoil. Set aside.

2. Combine the cheeses, flour, mustard, nutmeg, and chives in a bowl. Set aside.

3. Diagonally slice the sourdough loaf, making your cuts about an inch apart. Be careful to cut through the crumb while leaving the bottom and side crust intact. Now, slice diagonally in the opposite direction so you have a crisscross pattern.

4. Place the bacon and onion in a large pot over medium heat and sauté until the bacon is crispy. Remove the bacon mixture from the pot and set aside. Drain the fat into a glass jar to discard later.

5. Raise the heat to medium-high and add the beer and Worcestershire sauce to the now empty pot. When hot and just starting to boil, add the cheese mixture, a large handful at a time, until melted.

6. Place the bread on the prepared baking sheet.

7. Add the garlic to the melted butter and carefully pour or spoon into the crevices of the bread, followed by the bacon mixture and then the cheese mixture. This part is messy. That's A-OK! Go slowly and be prepared to lick cheese off your fingers.

8. Place in the hot oven and bake until bread is warmed through, 8 to 10 minutes.

9. Remove from the oven and top with chopped parsley.

10. Eat!

Brandy-Laced Chicken Liver Pâté

Serves: 4 to 6

INGREDIENTS

7 tablespoons unsalted
   butter

½ sweet onion, diced
   (½ cup)

2 garlic cloves, minced

9 ounces chicken livers

1 tablespoon chopped fresh
   thyme, plus extra sprigs

1 bay leaf

½ cup brandy

1 teaspoon red wine vinegar

Coarse sea salt and freshly
   ground black pepper

Whole peppercorns
   (optional)

1 batch Balsamicy Onions
   (page 219)

To garnish: toasted
   baguette

This appetizer is super quick to make; surprisingly affordable, considering what you'd shuck out at a restaurant for it; and totally delicious. I know spreadable meats aren't for everyone, but even non–liver eaters can get on board with this one.

INSTRUCTIONS

1. Melt 4 tablespoons of the butter in a large, nonstick frying pan over medium-low heat. When it starts to sizzle, add the onion and garlic and cook until translucent.

2. Add the chicken livers, chopped thyme, and bay leaf and cook for 5 to 7 minutes, until the livers are cooked through but not starting to brown.

3. Pour in the brandy, red wine vinegar, salt, and pepper and cook for about 2 minutes. Remove from the heat and discard the bay leaf.

4. Spoon the lot into a food processor or blender and process until smooth.

5. Pour into ramekins or short mason jars. Melt the remaining 3 tablespoons of butter and pour over the liver mixture to prevent oxidization. Gently garnish the tops with the Balsamicy Onions, thyme sprigs, and/or even a few whole peppercorns. Allow to sit for the butter to harden.

6. Serve on toasted baguettes or cover with plastic wrap and refrigerate until ready to use.

Tipsy Tip

Brandy is usually served after meals as a sipper, much like scotch or bourbon. But here we're serving it up premeal! Cognac (sweeter) or Armagnac (drier) would both be nice in this dish.

Vodka-Spiked Butternut Squash "Parcels" & Bloody Mary Tomato Jam

Yield: About 15 "parcels"

INGREDIENTS

One 2-pound butternut squash, peeled, seeded, and diced into ½-inch cubes

Coarse sea salt and freshly ground black pepper

Extra-virgin olive oil

40 fresh curry leaves, or 10 dried

1½ teaspoons black mustard seeds

½ teaspoon dried fenugreek seeds

1 onion, finely chopped

3 garlic cloves, minced

1½ inches fresh ginger, peeled and finely grated

1 tablespoon cumin seeds

1 teaspoon red pepper flakes

1 tablespoon ground cinnamon

½ cup vodka

1½ cups ricotta, drained

½ cup pine nuts, gently toasted

One 16-ounce package phyllo pastry sheets, defrosted

8 tablespoons (1 stick) unsalted butter, melted

1 batch Bloody Mary Tomato Jam (page 220)

This dish is adapted from a recipe by chef and author of *The Modern Vegetarian*, Maria Elia. It was the first time I'd ever cooked with Indian spices. I was so enamored with what came out of the oven, I was inspired to create my own boozy version. Bon appétit!

INSTRUCTIONS

1. Preheat your oven to 400°F. Arrange the squash on a large baking pan with a couple glugs of the oil and season with salt and black pepper. Toss well to coat and roast for about 25 minutes, or until soft. Remove from the oven and set aside.

2. Meanwhile, heat 2 to 3 tablespoons of the oil in a large frying pan over medium heat. Carefully add the curry leaves, mustard seeds, and fenugreek seeds and cook until they start to "pop."

3. Immediately add the onion, cumin seeds, garlic, ginger, red pepper flakes, and cinnamon and cook until the onion is softened, stirring occasionally.

4. Deglaze the pan with the vodka, being sure to scrape any stuck-on bits off the bottom. Simmer for 3 to 4 minutes, until most of the liquid has cooked off. Transfer to a bowl and let cool slightly.

5. Combine the cooked squash with the onion mixture, along with the ricotta and pine nuts. Adjust the seasoning to taste.

6. Preheat your oven to 350°F and line two baking sheets with parchment paper.

7. Lay out the phyllo sheets, keeping those you aren't working with covered with a damp tea towel so they don't dry out. Place one sheet of phyllo on a dry, flat, clean work surface, brush gently with melted butter starting from the center and making your way out toward the edges, and assertively place another sheet on top. Butter again and then cut lengthwise into four equal strips. Place a heaping tablespoon of the butternut mixture on the lower right-hand corner of each strip. Holding the top right-hand corner of the pastry, fold it over the mixture to form a triangular shape, having the edges meet. Then flip the triangle over to encase the mixture and continue this motion, lining up the edges all the way down the length of the phyllo. Seal the edges with butter and place on your prepared baking sheets. Brush the tops of each parcel with butter. Repeat until your baking sheets are full.

8. Place in the oven and bake for 25 minutes, or until crisp and golden.

9. When you put the parcels in the oven, start making your Bloody Mary Tomato Jam. Serve hot.

Tipsy Tip

The subtlety of the vodka in this dish is welcome because of the bolder flavors of the squash and tomatoes. But if you want to try something a little bit stronger, sub out the vodka for white rum, tequila, or even something herbaceous, such as aquavit.

Crunchy Pommes Frites with Madeira Balsamic Reduction

Serves: 4

INGREDIENTS

1 large russet potato, peeled and rinsed

Vegetable oil for frying

Coarse sea salt and freshly ground black pepper

1 batch Madeira Wine Balsamic Reduction (page 221)

To garnish: fresh lemon and roughly chopped fresh flat-leaf parsley

Tipsy Tip

You will have leftover Madeira Wine Balsamic Reduction—thank the bartending gods. Mix it into salad dressings or drizzle over other dishes, such as the Limoncello Shrimp (page 64) or Ale Stacked Mushrooms (page 160)!

When it comes to French fries, I am emphatically crunchy. I like 'em thin and crispy!

Serve these super crispy fries piled a mile high and with a sipper of the wine used for the balsamic reduction or a tall glass of prosecco. And then try to eat just a few—I dare you.

INSTRUCTIONS

1. Using a mandoline on the thinnest setting possible, julienne the potato superthin. Place the slices in a bowl of warm water and soak for 30 minutes to allow most of the starches to leach out. Dry very well with a tea towel, making sure to get all the excess moisture off, and set aside.

2. As the potatoes soak, make the Madeira Wine Balsamic Reduction.

3. Place a wire rack on top of a parchment-lined baking sheet and set aside.

4. Preheat your oven to 220°F.

5. Heat the vegetable oil in a deep wok or large, heavy-based pot (filled no more than one-third full) over medium heat until it reaches 350°F, or until a 1-inch cube of bread dropped into the oil browns in about 30 seconds. If it browns faster than that, turn down your heat—oil can combust if too hot and you don't want to break out the fire extinguisher! If it takes longer, then the oil hasn't come to temperature yet.

6. Using a spider skimmer or large slotted spoon, and cooking a handful-size batch at a time, carefully place the potato pieces in the oil, ensuring you don't splatter or burn your little fingers. Fry them for 6 to 8 minutes, remove with the skimmer, and place on the prepared rack. Try to spread them out a bit so the oil drains cleanly away from the fries. Season generously with salt and pepper. Place the finished fries in the oven to keep warm until the batch frying is finished.

7. Once all the potato pieces are fried, plate and drizzle with as much of the Madeira Wine Balsamic Reduction as you'd like and serve with fresh lemon and a sprinkling of parsley.

Verdejo Habas con Jamón (Fava Beans with Spanish Ham & Wine)

The first time I cooked fava beans (a.k.a. broad beans), I was taken aback by the time it took to shell the little green gems. Because they have two shells—the main outer shell and a rubbery casing inside—they're a labor of love, for sure. But since they're only around for a short two months a year, I make the effort. And am well rewarded. Trust me—they'll be your "fava-rites" for life.

INSTRUCTIONS

1. First, prepare the fava beans. This does take a bit of time, but it's very easy. Snap off the top end of each bean and gently peel off the seam (like shelling peas). Then gently wiggle your fingers inside to open the pod. Pop out the beans and discard the shells to the compost.

2. Now, here's the time-consuming part: the beans are tricky and have a second shell. You'll need to bring a large pot of water to a boil, dump the beans in, boil for 30 to 45 seconds to loosen the second casing, and then immediately drain and run cold water over the beans to stop the cooking process and maintain their brilliant green color. Now you can carefully make a tear in the outer coating near the "bum" of the bean (when you see them, you'll know what I mean) and just gently pinch the bean out of its casing. Ta-da! Bright green fava beans! Again, compost the shells.

3. Now's the easy part: Melt the butter in a large saucepan over medium heat. Add the onion, *jamón*, and garlic. Cook over medium heat for about 5 minutes, stirring often, until the onion softens.

4. Add the prepared fava beans and wine and cook over high heat until the liquid is reduced by half.

5. Add the stock, lower the heat to medium-low, cover, and cook for 10 minutes. Uncover and cook for another 10 minutes, or until the beans are tender and most of the liquid has evaporated, stirring occasionally. Season to taste with salt and pepper.

6. Serve hot and saddle up with some crusty bread to soak up the sauce. Enjoy!

Serves: 2 to 4

INGREDIENTS

4 pounds fava beans

2 tablespoons unsalted butter

1 yellow onion, diced (1 cup)

6 ounces *jamón* or *ibérico* ham (you can substitute smoked prosciutto if need be), chopped into ½-inch pieces

2 garlic cloves, minced

⅔ cup Verdejo Spanish wine

¾ cup chicken stock (page 224)

Coarse sea salt and freshly ground black pepper

Tipsy Tip

You will need many more beans than you think. Once the casings are gone, there is significantly less volume than when you first bought them. I recommend purchasing 1½ to 2 pounds unshelled favas per person.

There aren't many better things in the world than a damn good salad. Or soup, for that matter.

From the rustic and messy to the refined and elegant, soups and salads are something that can make or break a meal, as the course between courses or the main event.

When it's hot outside, they're refreshing and light—simple recipes for simple dinners when the last thing you want to do is turn on the oven, and the first thing you want to do is open a bottle of rosé and toast the sunshine. Tender & spicy arugula (page 83). Crunchy homemade croutons (page 84). Juicy watermelon (page 91).

In cold weather, they're more rustic. Messy. Delicious. Like a cozy oversize sweater or a good bottle of whiskey. Hearty, wilted greens (page 87). Warm spices (page 93). Oozy, decadent cheese and silky sauces (page 96).

Seasons aside, the soups and salads found here are something to be relished, consumed, and served in the most tempting way possible: with good friends.

soups & salads

Drunk Grilled Pear & Brie Salad   83

Mushroom Thyme Sherry Soup   84

Cauliflower, Kale, & Grapefruit Salad   87

Sangria Ajo Blanco (Spanish White Garlic Soup)   88

Mojito Watermelon Chopped Salad   91

Beef & Barley Red Wine Stew   93

Sparkling Rosé Roquefort Wedge Salad   95

Irish Whiskey French Onion Soup   96

Drunk Grilled Pear & Brie Salad

This was one of the last recipes developed for the book; it's also one of my favorites. Evidently you appreciate this combo, too, because my Prosciutto Arugula Salad Rolls on *She Eats* is one of the most popular recipes to date. Building on that super simple appetizer, I juiced up those little rolls and made an entire deconstructed platter out of them. Because, yum.

INSTRUCTIONS

1. Prepare the Drunk Pear Salad Dressing; set aside.

2. Preheat your grill to medium.

3. Place the lemon juice, oil, and pear liqueur in a bowl. Core and cut the pears into eighths lengthwise and "wash" in the mixture. This will help prevent the pears from browning and sticking to the grill.

4. When the grill is hot, shake the excess liquid off the pears and place on the grill, being careful not to move them until it's time to flip. This will make nice grill marks on the fruit. Cook for 2 to 3 minutes per side. They should be tender but not mushy.

5. Carefully remove the pears from the grill and let cool for 10 minutes.

6. Toss the cooled pears in a large bowl along with the arugula, almond slivers, salt and pepper, and a couple of tablespoons of the prepared dressing.

7. Gently stack on a large serving platter or individually into shallow bowls.

8. Add the cheese and gently tuck the prosciutto in among the leaves. If using, drizzle lightly with honey. Eat!

Serves: 4

INGREDIENTS

1 tablespoon lemon juice

2 teaspoons olive oil

1 teaspoon pear liqueur

2 pears (any variety, though Bosc and d'Anjou hold up to grilling better than Bartlett)

8 cups arugula

2 tablespoons toasted almond slivers

6 ounces Brie or Camembert, cut into ½-inch triangles (think of pie wedges)

Coarse sea salt and freshly ground black pepper

8 thin slices prosciutto

1 batch Drunk Pear Salad Dressing (page 221)

Optional: a little organic, local honey

Tipsy Tip

This is a fairly versatile salad, so feel free to swap out the fruit or greens for whatever's in season. Bitter dandelion greens are fabulous with the sweet fruit and dressing, while pears are delicious but so are apples and plums. In warmer weather, use blackberries, melon, or peaches. And if you don't have pear liqueur on hand, you can also substitute St-Germain (*holà!*) in this recipe or Calvados (apple brandy).

Mushroom Thyme Sherry Soup

Serves: 4 to 6

INGREDIENTS

5 tablespoons unsalted
  butter

3 large shallots, minced
  (½ cup)

3 garlic cloves, minced

1 pound fresh mushrooms
  (button, portobello,
  oyster, shiitakes, morels,
  or chanterelles are all
  good), chopped into ½-
  inch pieces

1 cup dry sherry

⅓ cup all-purpose flour

4 cups chicken, beef, or
  vegetable stock (page
  224)

1 teaspoon dried Italian
  seasoning

2 bay leaves

¼ cup roughly chopped
  fresh flat-leaf parsley

1 tablespoon fresh thyme
  leaves

Coarse sea salt

½ to ¾ cup heavy cream

Freshly ground black pepper

To garnish: chopped fresh
  chives and crusty bread

I've always savored mushroom soup. Especially a creamy one. There's something so comforting about it—like coming home on a cold fall afternoon to snuggle up with a book and your grandmother's blanket in front of a roaring fire.

This soup is hearty, soothing, and oh so rustic. It's like cooking up a delectable bowl of the forest floor and eating it. Mmmm . . . forest floor.

INSTRUCTIONS

1. Heat 2 tablespoons of the butter in a large, heavy-based pot over medium heat. When sizzling, add the shallots. Soften for 3 minutes. Stir in the garlic and cook for 1 minute, or until fragrant.

2. Add the mushrooms. Cook through, 12 to 15 minutes. If using more delicate mushrooms, such as shiitakes, morels, or chanterelles, lessen the cooking time by 5 minutes.

3. Pour in the sherry. Reduce for 2 minutes.

4. Stir in the remaining 3 tablespoons of butter and the flour and cook for 3 minutes to develop a roux (this will thicken your soup).

5. Whisk in the stock, Italian seasoning, herbs, and 2 teaspoons of salt. Bring to a light boil, lower the heat to low, and simmer, uncovered, for 25 minutes.

6. Remove from the heat and stir in the cream: If you like your soup more creamy, add it all; if you like less cream, only use about ½ cup.

7. Season to taste with salt and pepper.

8. Ladle into bowls and garnish with chopped chives. Serve with crusty bread.

Tipsy Tip

When buying sherry, spring for the midpriced bottle. For a few extra dollars you can get decent sherry that's actually quite delicious to drink on its own.

Cauliflower, Kale, & Grapefruit Salad

This salad is the exact opposite of boring. I often eat this salad as a huge vegetarian-friendly entrée with a little shaved Parmesan or as a side to a big, fat, grass-fed steak. I know it looks like a lot of spices, but trust me—once you get them all good and into the cauliflower, you'll be glad you bashed all those beautiful seeds.

Serves: 4

INGREDIENTS

1 large or 2 medium heads cauliflower, outer leaves removed

Coarse sea salt and freshly ground black pepper

1 tablespoon red pepper flakes

1 tablespoon cumin seeds

1 tablespoon coriander seeds

1 lemon

4 tablespoons olive oil

1 yellow onion, diced

1 large garlic clove, thinly sliced

1 large bunch kale, stemmed and chopped into 1-inch strips

¼ cup Crème de Pamplemousse Rose (grapefruit) liqueur or Campari plus 1 tablespoon grapefruit juice

Handful of flat-leaf parsley, roughly chopped

¼ cup oily black olives, pitted

¼ cup pine nuts, toasted

½ large grapefruit, peeled, seeded, and sectioned

Optional: freshly grated Parmesan

INSTRUCTIONS

1. Preheat your oven to 450°F.

2. Place the cauliflower on a cutting board, top-side up. With your chef's knife, slice the cauliflower down the middle. You should now have two pieces. Keeping the core intact, slice each half a second time in the exact same way, each piece about ½-inch thick. You should now have four cauliflower "steaks," plus the ends, per cauliflower head. Break the ends into florets.

3. Arrange them as a single layer on a shallow baking sheet and drizzle with 2 tablespoons of the oil. Season well with a pinch each of salt and pepper. Massage well to coat.

4. In a mortar and pestle (or spice grinder), bash the spices together with 1 teaspoon of salt—this helps act as an abrasive for the spices. When coarsely ground and fragrant, sprinkle the lot on both sides of the cauliflower. Squeeze lemon juice over it all. Roast in the oven for 20 to 30 minutes, flipping halfway through, until the cauliflower is tender and browned.

5. As the cauliflower roasts, pour the remaining 2 tablespoons of oil into a large frying pan over medium heat.

6. When the oil is shimmering hot but not smoking, add the onion. Cook for about 5 minutes, stirring regularly. Add the garlic, wait a minute, and then toss in the kale. Season with salt and pepper and stir well. Cover and allow the kale to become dark green and glossy, approximately 5 minutes.

7. Remove the lid and pour in the Pamplemousse liqueur. Reduce until the liquid has gone but the flavor has coated the kale.

8. Chuck the kale on a big ole serving platter and arrange the cauliflower among it. Top with the parsley, olives, pine nuts, and grapefruit wedges and, if using, grated Parmesan. Eat.

Sangria Ajo Blanco
(Spanish White Garlic Soup)

Serves: 4

INGREDIENTS

2 cups water

2½ cups cubed day-old white bread (crust removed and discarded—or eaten—and cut into 1-inch cubes)

2 to 3 medium garlic cloves, peeled

1½ cups untoasted slivered almonds

½ cup dry Spanish (ideally Catalan) white wine

2 tablespoons St-Germain, pear liqueur, or Calvados

½ cup extra-virgin olive oil

2 tablespoons sherry or white wine vinegar

Coarse sea salt

1 cup mixed fruit of your choosing: pitted cherries, peach or nectarine slices, sliced kiwi, berries, chopped apple, halved grapes, plum wedges, watermelon cubes

⅓ cup toasted slivered almonds

I've bastardized traditional *ajo blanco* (Spanish white garlic soup) in a good way here by adding wine, liqueur, and lots of fresh fruit. It's sangria in soup form. And totally invigorating on those hot summer days when you just can't bear to turn the oven on. Or you've had too much wine to do so. Enjoy with good friends and unruly laughter.

INSTRUCTIONS

1. Make the soup base: Place the water, bread, garlic, and untoasted almonds in your food processor. Puree on high speed until smooth.

2. With the motor running, add the white wine, liqueur, oil, vinegar, and 1 tablespoon of sea salt. Emulsify. Taste. If desired, add more salt.

3. Place the soup base in the fridge for 2 to 3 hours to chill completely.

4. To serve, ladle into shallow bowls and garnish with fruit of your choosing and toasted slivered almonds. Eat!

Tipsy Tip

This recipe makes a particularly thick soup that I tend to serve as an appetizer at summer BBQs and dinner parties. But if you want a larger bowl as a main entrée, you may want to thin it out a bit. If so, add more water, ¼ cup at a time, until the soup reaches the desired consistency.

Mojito Watermelon Chopped Salad

This salad is a fusion of Cuba and Spain—two Latin cultures near and dear to my heart. And clearly my plate.

Mojito ingredients—a Cuban cocktail composed of white rum, sugar, lime juice, sparkling water, and mint—give the dish a surprising brightness, while Spanish Marcona almonds—round, plump, and delicate—give it a satisfying crunchy yet creamy note. Together, they're one punchy combination that makes this dish one of my go-tos come summertime.

INSTRUCTIONS

1. Prepare the salad dressing; set aside.

2. Chuck the watermelon in a bowl along with most of the mint, feta, almonds, and all of the dressing. Mix well.

3. Garnish with any remaining mint, feta, almonds, and the lime zest.

4. The longer this salad sits, the better. It can be made up to 6 hours in advance. Eat.

Serves: 4

INGREDIENTS

4 cups watermelon, chopped into 1-inch pieces (from 1 small to medium watermelon)

Handful of fresh mint leaves, thinly sliced

1 cup drained and crumbled feta

½ cup Marcona almonds

1 batch Mojito Watermelon Salad Dressing (page 222)

Zest of 1 lime

Tipsy Tip

Going to a par-tay? Make this salad graze-friendly by allowing the watermelon to soak in the dressing for a few hours before draining and serving on cocktail sticks. Garnish with the remaining salad ingredients and bon appétit!

Beef & Barley Red Wine Stew

Serves: 10

INGREDIENTS

Virgin olive oil

3 pounds chuck beef, cut
into 1-inch pieces

Coarse sea salt and freshly
ground black pepper

2 cups chopped carrot
(2-inch pieces)

3 medium celery stalks,
chopped into ½-inch
pieces

1 sweet onion, chopped

5 garlic cloves, minced

1½ cups dry red wine

4 cups beef stock (page
224)

One 28-ounce can diced
tomatoes

1 tablespoon Worcestershire
sauce

2 bay leaves

2 tablespoons chopped
fresh rosemary

2 tablespoon chopped fresh
thyme

Parmesan rind (optional)

1 pound waxy potatoes,
chopped into 1-inch
pieces

1 cup pearl barley

1½ cups frozen peas

When it comes to stew and soups, I like to make a lot. Like, a lot. And this makes a TON of stew, which is lucky because it's rich, sultry, and oh so lustrous, yet simple enough to make regularly. It's on my weekly rotation!

If this is too much stew for you, freeze half for an easy defrost-and-reheat weekday meal or halve the recipe to make a smaller batch.

INSTRUCTIONS

1. Heat a large pot over medium-high heat. Once hot, drizzle with a tablespoon of oil and add the beef pieces—you may have to do this in batches so you don't crowd the pan (if the pan is crowded, you'll steam the meat rather than brown it). Brown well all over, seasoning generously with salt and pepper. Remove from the pot and set aside.

2. Once the beef is browned, lower the heat to medium. Add a couple glugs of oil to the pan, if necessary, and add the carrots, celery, and onion. Stir well to coat. Cook for about 5 minutes, or until just starting to get a bit of color on the vegetables, stirring occasionally. Add the garlic and cook for 1 minute.

3. Pour in the wine to deglaze the pan—be sure to scrape up any bits stuck there. Allow the wine to reduce for 2 to 3 minutes.

4. Add the beef stock, tomatoes, bay leaf, Worcestershire, rosemary, and thyme. Season well with salt and pepper. If you have a Parmesan rind on hand, now is the time to add that, too. Place the beef back in the pot.

5. Bring to a boil over high heat. Cover, lower the heat to a low simmer, and slow cook for 2½ to 3 hours.

6. When there's 45 minutes left on the timer, uncover and add the potatoes and barley.

7. In the final 5 minutes of cooking, stir in the frozen peas.

8. Before serving, season to taste and remove the bay leaves and any remaining Parmesan rind.

Note

There are dozens of types of barley available. Use pearl barley (the husk and bran layer are removed for quick cooking), which tastes slightly nutty and readily absorbs the flavors of the stew. Hulled and pot barley could also work, but take longer to cook and are denser and chewier.

Sparkling Rosé Roquefort Wedge Salad

We all need to get over the idea that iceberg lettuce is hideous. Is it dated? Yes. Tacky? A little bit. But totally, fabulously, and deliciously retro? Hells yeah.

Think about it—if thick black-rimmed glasses, lumberjack beards, Pyrex bowls, knitting, mason jars, and crop tops can make a comeback, there's no reason iceberg lettuce can't too. I declare we make iceberg lettuce the official lettuce of hipsters everywhere. Are ya with me?

With a ton of texture and butt-loads of flavor, this salad is playful on the plate and playful on the palate. Sparkling rosé is one of my favorite kinds of wine—it keeps things light, not too serious, and totally sexy.

Not unlike black-rimmed glasses, lumberjack beards, and crop tops.

INSTRUCTIONS

1. Prepare the quick pickled onions and dressing; set aside.

2. Set a large frying pan over medium heat and add the bacon. Cook for about 12 minutes, or until brown and crispy, stirring occasionally. Remove from the pan with a slotted spoon and drain on paper towels. Carefully spoon 1 tablespoon of the bacon fat into the bowl of your food processor or blender for the dressing.

3. Leaving the rest of the fat in the pan, add the chopped bread and raise the heat to medium-high. Coat well with the fat and allow the croutons to toast and brown. When golden and dry, remove from the heat and set aside.

4. To serve: Place a wedge of lettuce on each person's plate. Drizzle a quarter of the dressing over the lettuce. Top with the chives, crumbled blue cheese, croutons, bacon, a pinch of flaky sea salt and pepper, and a small handful of the pickled onions. Eat.

Serves: 4

INGREDIENTS

8 ounces bacon, chopped

4 (1-inch-thick) slices of day-old crusty bread, cut into ½-inch cubes

1 head iceberg lettuce, rough outer leaves discarded, cut into quarters

½ cup fresh chives, finely chopped

½ cup crumbled Roquefort blue cheese

Flaky sea salt

Freshly ground black pepper

1 batch Quick Pickled Onions (page 228)

1 batch Sparkling Rosé Roquefort Dressing (page 223)

Tipsy Tip

When it comes to wedge salad, the more dressing, the better. Generously get it all in the cracks of the lettuce—don't be afraid. The crisp lettuce and pickled onions cut through the richness of the blue cheese and make for a well-balanced—if not orgasmic—mouthful, each and every bite.

Irish Whiskey French Onion Soup

Serves: 4 to 6

INGREDIENTS

5 tablespoons unsalted butter

4 pounds sweet onions, peeled and thinly sliced

Coarse sea salt

3 garlic cloves, minced

2 tablespoons fresh thyme leaves, chopped

1 cup Irish whiskey

8 cups beef stock (page 224)

Freshly ground black pepper

1 tablespoon olive oil

2 ciabatta or sourdough buns, halved

2 cups grated Gruyère

Tipsy Tip

Many French onion soups use red wine in lieu of whiskey and you can do that here if you don't have whiskey on hand. But I like using whiskey because (a) it's whiskey, and (b) Julia Child used to throw a splash of hard liquor in hers, too. And that chick knew good food.

This soup is damn good. The key is to give the onions time to really slowly caramelize so I suggest you don't rush them. Something happens to onions when they're given a nice, slow heat—they transform, becoming rich in flavor and decadent in texture. The thyme in this recipe practically melts into the onions, while the whiskey adds a full roundness to the broth. Plus, lots of Gruyère. Obvi.

INSTRUCTIONS

1. Melt 4 tablespoons of the butter in a large stockpot over medium-low heat. When hot, add the onions and a generous pinch of salt. Stir well and slowly sauté until golden and caramelized, stirring often. This should take 45 to 60 minutes. If your pot isn't big enough, do this in two batches, using 2 tablespoons of butter per batch. If caramelizing in two batches, add the first batch back to the pot before moving on to the next step.

2. Add the garlic and thyme and cook, stirring constantly, for about 1 minute.

3. When fragrant, deglaze the pot with the Irish whiskey and allow to simmer for about a minute to cook away some of the alcohol.

4. Add the beef stock, a generous grinding of pepper, and additional salt to taste. Stir well. Bring to a boil and then lower the heat to low, cover and simmer for 90 minutes, stirring occasionally. Stir in the remaining 1 tablespoon of butter. Be sure to taste the soup before serving—don't be shy about adding more salt or pepper if it needs more "punch."

5. When there are about 15 minutes left for the soup, preheat your oven broiler. Gently brush the cut side of the bread with the olive oil and place under the heating element to toast—watch to make sure the bread doesn't burn!

6. When the bread gets crispy and golden, top with half of the cheese. Place back under the broiler element for a few seconds to melt, then remove from the heat and set aside.

7. To serve, pour a couple of big ladles of the soup into a deep bowl, topping with the cheese toasts and remaining cheese. Enjoy!

The next time you go to the butcher or farmers' market, ask these four questions and then make the best decision for you:

Is the meat local?

Typically, local producers who are raising animals sustainably and ethically will let you visit to check out the farm, so you can see for yourself how the animals and workers are treated. Plus buying local supports your local economy, is good for your wallet, and is less harmful to the environment.

How was the animal raised?

If it was in a pasture, you're good to go! The next-best option is free-range. Ideally you want the animals to spend their life living their innate "cowness", "chickenness," or "pig-ness," as Joel Salatin says. This makes for flavorful and happy animals.

What was the animal fed?

Pasture-raised animals generally feed on a simple diet of what they've evolved to eat—that is, what they find in the pasture. Grass, hay, bugs, silage. Pigs and chickens typically eat some grain, too. Avoid "grain-fed" on beef labels, though. While it means the animal received a vegetarian diet free of animal parts and by-products, the animal can still get sick, and it's not good for the environment.

How was the animal slaughtered?

Generally, *kosher* or *halal* means the animal was killed in the most-humane and least-stressful way possible. Buy directly from small farmers at the market or a reputable butcher to find this kind of meat.

See? That wasn't so bad. Now go pour yourself a big-girl glass of wine and eat!

meaty

Cuervo & Tecate Pork Carnitas   100

Stout Blue Cheese Bison Burgers   103

Baked Acorn Squash, Radicchio, & Lamb
Merguez with Sweet Vermouth   105

Apple Cider Roasted Pork Loin   108

Sherry Ragu with Rabbit & Pappardelle
Noodles   111

Chocolate Porter-Marinated Lamb Pops with
Pea, Mint, & Feta "Salad"   114

Maple Whiskey-Laced BBQ Meatballs   117

Grilled Flank Steak with Bordelaise Sauce   118

Lager-Simmered Chicken Thighs   121

Rob Roy Braised Short Ribs   122

Cuervo & Tecate Pork Carnitas

Serves: 4 to 6

INGREDIENTS

4 pounds pork shoulder or butt, trimmed of excess fat and cut into 2-inch pieces

1 medium onion, chopped

5 large garlic cloves, peeled and smashed with the back of a knife

Zest and juice of 1 orange

Zest and juice of 2 limes

1 tablespoon tomato paste

2 teaspoons cumin seeds

2 teaspoons dried oregano

2 bay leaves

2 chipotle peppers in adobo sauce plus 1 tablespoon adobo sauce

1 tall-boy can Tecate

⅓ cup Cuervo

1 cup chicken, beef, or vegetable stock (page 224)

1 tablespoon coarse sea salt

1 teaspoon freshly ground black pepper

This recipe was inspired by one of my favorite (country) musicians, Brad Paisley, and has since become my annual birthday dinner. The active prep/cooking time is minimal and it's a dish that's brimming with flavor. It's a taco party waiting to happen. Have plenty of good tequila and beer to wash it all down.

INSTRUCTIONS

1. Place all the ingredients in a slow cooker and stir to combine. Ensure most of the ingredients are covered with liquid. Cover, set the temperature at LOW, and let cook for 7 hours.

2. Place a strainer over a large bowl and strain the liquid from the solids. Be careful—it's hot! Reserving the solids inside the strainer, transfer the liquid to a medium saucepan over medium-high heat. If desired, puree the strained vegetables—not the meat—in a food processor and add back to the liquid. Set meat aside.

3. Bring to a boil, lower the heat to medium-low, and simmer to reduce to 1 cup.

4. As the liquid reduces, remove the meat from the strainer and shed with a fork.

5. When the sauce has reduced, add the meat to the pot to heat through. You can also heat your tortillas at this time and get your sides ready.

6. Assemble with: tortillas, avocado, feta or Cotija, fresh cilantro, green onion, lime wedges, Quick Pickled Onions (page 228), hot sauces. Enjoy!

Stout Blue Cheese Bison Burgers

Unlike beef, farmed bison is less meaty tasting and therefore carries other flavors really well. I like to add caramelized onions to mine along with blue cheese—a sweet and savory match that pairs better than a left and right shoe. Plus the added fat from the blue cheese helps the lean bison retain some moisture. As a good friend of mine describes it, this is an epic BBQ meal!

Serves: 4

INSTRUCTIONS

1. Prepare the Smoky Stout BBQ Sauce and Quick Pickled Onions; set aside.

2. Drizzle the olive oil into a frying pan over medium heat. When hot but not smoking, add the onion. Sauté, stirring often, until golden and caramelized, about 30 minutes.

3. Add the garlic, stir. Cook for 1 minute, or until fragrant.

4. Pour the lot into a large mixing bowl and allow to cool slightly.

5. Preheat your BBQ grill to 500°F and line a large plate with parchment paper.

6. Add the bison, blue cheese, thyme leaves, Worcestershire, stout beer, egg, ¾ cup of the bread crumbs, and a generous helping of salt and pepper to the onion bowl. Mix well with your hands to combine. If you need a few more bread crumbs, go ahead and add the rest. Be careful not to overhandle, or you'll end up with tough burgers.

7. Divide the mixture into four equal-size balls and shape into ½-inch patties. Place on the prepared plate and press your thumb into the center of each one to create a 1-inch-wide impression—this helps to keep them flat while they cook.

8. Rub the outside of each patty on all sides with a little of the vegetable oil to coat. This keeps the burgers from sticking on the grill.

9. Place on the BBQ grill, close the lid, and cook for 5 minutes, flip, close the lid, and then cook for another 4 minutes.

continued

INGREDIENTS

1 tablespoon extra-virgin olive oil

1 medium yellow onion, diced (1 cup)

3 garlic cloves, minced

1 pound ground bison

½ cup crumbled blue cheese

2 teaspoons fresh thyme leaves

2 teaspoons Worcestershire sauce

¼ cup stout beer

1 large egg

¾ to 1 cup fine bread crumbs

Coarse sea salt and freshly ground black pepper

A little vegetable oil

4 brioche burger buns

1 batch Quick Pickled Onions (page 228)

1 batch Smoky Stout BBQ Sauce (page 227)

To serve: your favorite burger fixin's! Along with the Quick Pickled Onions and Smoky Stout BBQ Sauce, I like crunchy lettuce, yellow mustard, sliced avocado, and more blue cheese.

When you go to cook your burgers, do *not* press them on the grates with a spatula. Place them, close the lid, and let them sit for the allocated cooking time. Flip. Repeat. When you press a burger as it cooks, you push out all the moisture, and since bison is already lean, you could end up with dry burgers.

10. When there's 1 minute left on the timer, slather the top of each burger with the Smoky Stout BBQ Sauce.

11. Remove from the grill and let rest for 2 minutes before serving. As they rest, toast the brioche buns on the top rack of the BBQ grill.

12. Serve with your favorite burger fixin's. Enjoy!

Baked Acorn Squash, Radicchio, & Lamb Merguez with Sweet Vermouth

Winter squash has a thick skin perfect for showcasing the ingredients in this dish. It's a real wow factor. But more so than the presentation, the flavors in this recipe are holy amazing! Sweet, salty, spicy, bitter, smoky, and savory. And the textures are well rounded—soft squash, crunchy walnuts, chewy sausage. You will love it love it love it.

Serves: 4

INGREDIENTS

2 medium acorn squash

4 tablespoons (½ stick) unsalted butter, at room temperature

2 teaspoons coarse sea salt, plus more for seasoning vermouth mixture

2 tablespoons dark brown sugar

4 teaspoons pure maple syrup

2 spiced lamb sausages, casings removed, broken into 1-inch pieces

1 cup sweet vermouth

1 chipotle pepper in adobo sauce, chopped

1 small head radicchio, quartered, stemmed, and leaves separated

¼ cup roughly torn fresh mint leaves

⅓ cup chopped walnuts, toasted

1 batch Spiced Yogurt Sauce (page 225)

INSTRUCTIONS

1. Prepare the Spiced Yogurt Sauce; set aside.

2. Preheat your oven to 350°F. Carefully—and with a very sharp chef's knife—cut the squash in half from top to bottom. Scoop out the insides and discard so you're left with four clean halves.

3. Score the squash diagonally with a paring knife, cutting through the flesh but not the skin. Now score it again the opposite direction, so you have a crisscross pattern.

4. Divide the butter into four equal portions and rub all over the inside of the halves, followed by equal portions of the salt, brown sugar, and maple syrup.

5. Fill a roasting pan with ½ inch of hot water. Place the squash, cut side up, in the prepared roasting pan. Carefully place in the hot oven and bake for 1 hour, or until the squash is very tender and golden. There will be some syrupy liquid left in the squash. Feel free to spoon that into the scored areas when you pull it out of the oven.

6. With 20 minutes left on the squash, prepare the rest of the dish: Place a medium frying pan over medium heat. When hot, add the lamb sausage. Sauté, stirring regularly, until browned and cooked through, 7 to 10 minutes. Remove the sausage from the pan with a slotted spoon or fine metal strainer and set aside. Drain the fat out of the pan.

7. Place the pan back over medium heat and deglaze with the vermouth. Be careful—it may spit and sputter. Be sure to scrape any stuck-on bits from the bottom of the pan. These = flavor!

continued

8. Add the chipotle pepper and season with a little salt. Allow the mixture to reduce by about half.

9. By now the squash should be finished. Remove from the oven. Set aside two halves. Scoop out the other two halves and add to the vermouth mixture along with the radicchio leaves, toasted walnuts, and cooked sausage. Toss well and allow the radicchio to wilt slightly.

10. To serve: With a large spoon, smear the spiced yogurt on two plates. This will add flavor and also help hold your squash in place. Gently place the reserved squash "bowls" on top. Fill with the sausage mixture and top with mint leaves.

Tipsy Tip

If you want to crank it up a notch—and we all do—toast the seeds from the squash and garnish the dish with them right before serving! Now *that* is presentation! Whole animal cuisine? Nay, whole vegetable.

Apple Cider Roasted Pork Loin

This is the dish featured on the cover of the book. It's vintage and classy—a throw-down to the meals that nourish us, both literally and figuratively. It's also loaded with an apple flavor and aroma that stirs something in my loins. Paired with fresh herbs, dried spices, and so much apple, it's as if the farm—and those who produced the ingredients—are right there with us.

INGREDIENTS

1½ pounds pork loin

2 cups Brussels sprouts, cleaned and halved

2 cups chopped carrot (1-inch pieces)

1 yellow onion, chopped (1 cup)

2 celery sticks, chopped (½ cup)

2 cups chopped waxy potatoes (1½-inch pieces)

5 garlic cloves, peeled and smashed with the flat side of a knife

2 tablespoons chopped fresh thyme leaves

2 tablespoons chopped fresh rosemary leaves

1 tablespoon extra-virgin olive oil

Coarse sea salt and freshly ground black pepper

2 tablespoons coriander seeds

1 tablespoon cumin seeds

2 tablespoons unsalted butter

2 cups dry hard apple cider

INSTRUCTIONS

1. Remove the pork loin from the fridge 30 to 45 minutes before you're ready to cook it so the center isn't supercold and it cooks evenly.

2. When ready to cook, preheat your oven to 425°F.

3. Mix together the Brussel sprouts, carrot, yellow onion, celery, potatoes, garlic, thyme, and rosemary in a roasting pan. Drizzle with the oil and season with salt and pepper to taste. Mix well.

4. Bash the coriander seeds and cumin seeds with a pinch of salt in a mortar and pestle (or spice grinder). Spread out over a cutting board. Set aside.

5. Gently pat the pork loin dry of any excess moisture, using a paper towel, and season all sides generously with sea salt and pepper. Roll the pork through the cracked spices, making sure all sides get evenly crusted.

6. Set a sauté pan on medium-high heat. Add 1 tablespoon of the butter. When sizzling and hot, place the prepared pork loin in the center and sear well on all sides. Don't worry if the meat is longer than the pan; just curve it so it fits. When well browned on all sides, place the pork on top of the prepared vegetables.

7. Deglaze the sauté pan with the apple cider, scraping any stuck-on bits off the bottom, and allow to reduce by about half. Gently pour over the meat, cover the roasting pan, and place in the oven. Roast for 30 minutes. At that mark, remove the lid and roast for a further 15 to 20 minutes, until cooked through and the internal temperature of the meat at its thickest area reads 145°F.

continued

If you really want to play up the apples in this recipe, sauté a few apple slices as the meat rests. Place 1 tablespoon of butter in a small frying pan over medium-high heat. When sizzling, toss in cored, ½-inch-thick apple slices and warm through—you may even get a bit of caramelization happening on them. Serve alongside the sliced pork loin and sauce.

8. Remove the roasting pan from the oven. Set the meat on a wire rack and cover with tinfoil to rest for 20 minutes, and transfer the veg to a serving platter. Cover to keep warm.

9. While the meat rests, pour the drippings into the original sauté pan. Place over medium-high heat and reduce to about ½ cup of liquid. If your pork didn't have a lot of drippings, you may not need to reduce it too much. Stir in the remaining tablespoon of butter and season to taste.

10. Cut the pork into ¼- to ½-inch-thick slices and serve with the roasted veg and sauce. Enjoy!

Sherry Ragu with Rabbit & Pappardelle Noodles

Let's get one thing out of the way right here and now: Rabbits are adorable. So cute. They're also deliriously tasty. In fact, if I was on death row and was offered one final meal, this would be it. I know, I'm setting the expectations kind of high here, aren't I?

Let's start over: This recipe is a'ight.

The flavor of rabbit is similar to that of chicken but slightly sweeter and just barely gamey. Slow roasted and then served up on a big plate of pasta, it is by far a fabulous and delicious way to spend a Saturday night.

INSTRUCTIONS

1. Drizzle ¼ cup of the oil into a large stockpot over medium heat. As it warms, season the rabbit on all sides with salt and black pepper. When the pan is hot, add the rabbit and brown on all sides. Remove from the pot and set aside.

2. Add the onion, carrot, and celery. Sauté until starting to caramelize, stirring often.

3. Once the veggies start to get a bit of color on them, add the garlic and tomato paste. Massage into the mixture and allow to darken slightly, stirring constantly.

4. Add the sherry to deglaze the pan, making sure to scrape any stuck-on bits free for flavor!

5. After 3 minutes, add the chicken stock, crushed tomatoes, balsamic vinegar, bay leaves, thyme, rosemary, red pepper flakes, and rabbit. Raise the heat to high to bring to a boil, then lower the heat to a medium-low simmer and let bubble away for 1½ to 2 hours.

6. Place a fine-mesh colander over a large bowl and carefully drain the pot through the sieve. Using tongs, pull the rabbit meat out of the mixture and set aside. You may need to stir the lot to push all the liquid through the holes. Discard everything but the liquid and meat.

7. Pour the new, clean liquid back into the pot and allow it to reduce for 30 to 40 minutes.

Serves: 4

INGREDIENTS

Virgin olive oil

1 large organic rabbit, sectioned

Coarse sea salt and freshly ground black pepper

1 medium onion, diced (½ cup)

1 large carrot, diced (½ cup)

2 celery stalks, diced (½ cup)

3 garlic cloves, minced

¼ cup tomato paste

2 cups medium-dry or dry sherry

3 cups chicken stock (page 224)

One 28-ounce can crushed San Marzano tomatoes

3 tablespoons balsamic vinegar

2 bay leaves

3 sprigs fresh thyme

3 sprigs fresh rosemary

1 teaspoon red pepper flakes

One 8-ounce package of pappardelle noodles

2 tablespoons unsalted butter

continued

8. As that reduces, gently shred the rabbit meat off the bones. Be careful—the bones of a rabbit are teeny-tiny and you want to get them all. Discard the bones and return the meat to the simmering liquid. If desired, rabbit can be made up to 2 days in advance.

9. When there's 15 minutes left on the simmer, bring a large pot of generously salted water to a boil. Add the pappardelle noodles. Cook until al dente, drain, and then add the noodles to the meaty sauce along with the butter. Mix well.

10. If desired, serve topped with a few shavings of fresh Parmesan. Enjoy!

Tipsy Tip

I learned how to section a rabbit for this recipe. Without a meat cleaver. That was interesting. If I were you, I'd ask your butcher to do this for you, so you don't ruin your knives.

Chocolate Porter-Marinated Lamb Pops with Pea, Mint, & Feta "Salad"

Serves: 4

INGREDIENTS

2 cups chocolate porter

1 tablespoon chopped fresh
  rosemary leaves

1 tablespoon chopped fresh
  thyme leaves

2 to 3 garlic cloves, minced
  (1 tablespoon)

2 teaspoons good-quality
  balsamic vinegar

¼ cup olive oil

Coarse sea salt and freshly
  ground black pepper

1 French-cut rack of lamb,
  trimmed of excess fat and
  cut into 8 chops

3 tablespoons vegetable oil

2 cups shelled garden peas

½ cup drained and
  crumbled feta

¼ cup roughly torn fresh
  mint leaves

To serve: crusty bread

Tipsy Tip

If you can't find a chocolate
porter, substitute a chocolate
stout. Either way, you'll obtain
the rich, sweet, velvety flavor
and texture of the marinade
and sauce.

I had a friend tell me that this is the first dish he's going to make when the book comes out. His words:

"This lamb is perfect for any time of the year, and it has a major wow factor. The lamb was moist and the flavor was great and the peas were shockingly good. I think it took a total of 17 seconds to eat the entire meal because I inhaled it. Marinating it made it the perfect choice for a weekend where you have other things to do and can set it and forget it. This is great for summer days when you don't want to be in the kitchen but want an amazing meal."

Okay, H. I'm convinced. Dish me up.

INSTRUCTIONS

1. Combine the porter, rosemary, thyme, garlic, vinegar, olive oil, and salt and pepper to taste in a shallow baking dish. Add the lamb. Place in the fridge and marinate for 4 to 5 hours. Remove from the fridge 30 minutes before you're ready to cook.

2. Place a wire rack on a cutting board. Set aside.

3. Set a pan on medium-high heat and drizzle with the vegetable oil. When hot but not smoking, shake off the excess marinade from the lamb and sear 3 minutes per side. Remove from the pan and place on the wire rack. Cover with foil and let rest for 5 minutes.

4. As the meat rests, turn the heat to medium and pour ¾ cup of the marinade into the hot pan. Be careful—it'll spit and splatter a bit.

5. Toss in the garden peas and poach until cooked through, about 5 minutes. The liquid should also reduce to create a meaty, sweet glaze on the peas. Remove from the heat and scatter with the feta and mint leaves. Season to taste.

6. Spoon the mixture onto a big serving plate and top with the lamb, family style. Serve with crusty bread. Enjoy!

Maple Whiskey-Laced BBQ Meatballs

I'm a firm believer that making meatballs is an art form that needs to be honed and perfected. There are a lot of factors to consider when shaping a meatball: Texture, flavor, moisture, the crust, the kind of meat to use and the ratio, the type of bread crumbs, the herbs, accent flavor profiles and seasonings, and the integrity of the egg to bind it all together; a lot of love goes into a good one. And clearly a lot of whiskey.

I have yet to figure out how many of these you need to eat to get a buzz. But they're so damn good, you may want to figure it out on your own.

INSTRUCTIONS

1. Prepare the BBQ sauce; set aside.

2. Put the flour in a shallow bowl and line a large plate with parchment paper. Set aside.

3. Place all the remaining ingredients, except the oil, in a large mixing bowl. Using your hands, mix well to combine, being careful not to overwork the meat.

4. Roll the meat into 1 1/2-inch balls and then gently toss in the flour—this helps the balls stay together during cooking and creates a good crust on the outside. Shake off the excess flour and place on the pre-pared plate.

5. Once all balls are formed, preheat your oven to 350°F.

6. Heat the oil in a large, oven-safe pan. When the oil is hot, add the balls and carefully shake to coat with the oil. Brown well on all sides. Be careful not to crowd the pan, or you'll steam the balls rather than brown them; you may need to do this in batches if your pan isn't large enough.

7. Cover the pan and place in the hot oven for 12 to 15 minutes.

8. To serve, coat with the Smoky Maple Whiskey BBQ Sauce and heat through, if necessary.

Yield: 14 meatballs

INGREDIENTS

¾ cup all-purpose flour

8 ounces ground beef

8 ounces ground pork

1 large, egg

1 small onion, finely diced

2 garlic cloves, minced

1 tablespoon finely chopped fresh flat-leaf parsley

¼ teaspoon ground allspice

4 good dashes Worcestershire sauce

½ cup panko bread crumbs

1 teaspoon coarse sea salt

1 teaspoon freshly ground pepper

2 tablespoons vegetable oil

1 batch Smoky Maple Whiskey BBQ Sauce (page 227)

Tipsy Tip

This is true of hamburgers as much as it is of meatballs—cook the onions and brown them thoroughly before mixing with the meat for a softer, less oniony flavor. Sometimes I do this; sometimes I can't be bothered. See which level of "onionyness" works for you.

Grilled Flank Steak with Bordelaise Sauce

Serves: 4 to 5

INGREDIENTS

Coarse sea salt and freshly ground black pepper

2½ pounds flank steak

1 tablespoon vegetable oil

1 batch Bordelaise Sauce (page 229)

Tipsy Tip

Steak and mushrooms is a classic! To serve mushrooms on the side of yours and make this a complete dish, throw a bit of butter and some quartered mushrooms into a pan over medium heat and brown all over while the steak rests. If you start them a bit earlier while the steak is on the grill, you could even deglaze the pan with a splash of Bordeaux to tie it all together. Just let the wine simmer and absorb into the mushrooms for the last 3 to 4 minutes of cooking.

When it comes to steak, I'm generally a salt-and-pepper-only kinda gal. I don't like to muddy up the terrain with additional flavors (a.k.a. distractions). But I'll be honest: this Bordelaise Sauce is kind of insanity. Whether you're a seasoned chef or an al dente home cook, you'll find it's easy, elegant, and totally perfect to fancy up your steak.

INSTRUCTIONS

1. Remove the steak from the fridge 30 minutes before you're ready to cook.

2. As it comes to room temperature, begin the Bordelaise Sauce.

3. Place a cast-iron pan over medium-high heat *or* preheat your grill (my favorite!) to 450°F. As the element heats, rub the steak with the vegetable oil—this keeps excess oil in the pan from smoking but will still help you get a good even sear on the meat. Season generously with salt and pepper on both sides.

4. Place the steak on the heat and cook until it reaches your desired doneness. You don't want to cook a flank steak the whole way through, or you'll end up with one stiff, dry piece of meat. Shoot for medium rare, about 6 minutes per side, or until the meat reaches 135° to 140°F on a meat thermometer. And please, for the love of all that is delicious and meaty, don't move the steak around—every time you lift it or shift it, you're reducing the sear. Sear = flavor!

5. Remove from the heat, transfer to a wire rack to allow the air to circulate around the meat, which distributes the juices evenly, and cover with tinfoil. Let rest 10 minutes.

6. To serve the steak, place the rested meat on a cutting board, and using a very sharp knife, slice against the grain (perpendicular) so as to make the fibers of the steak shorter. This will make the meat more tender. Spoon a few tablespoons of sauce onto a plate and top with the meat. Garnish with an extra herb sprig, if desired.

Lager-Simmered Chicken Thighs

I won't lie—I don't cook a lot of chicken. I prefer bolder, more confident flavors than what flies with chicken.

But there are exceptions to the rule, of course—isn't there always? And I'm of the firm assertion that bone-in dark chicken meat, simmered in beer and finished with cream, is fantastic. It's even better the second day as the flavors have a chance to meld.

INSTRUCTIONS

1. Heat a large frying pan over medium-heat.

2. Add the chopped bacon and cook until crispy, 12 to 15 minutes. Remove from the pan with a slotted spoon and set aside.

3. Season the chicken amply with salt and pepper. Arrange, skin side down, in the pan of bacon fat and cook until browned and crispy. Flip to brown the bottom and then remove from the pan and set aside with the bacon. Discard all but 4 tablespoons of the fat.

4. Add the onion and carrots to the pan and sauté until soft. Add the garlic, stirring for about a minute, and then the mushrooms. Stir and continue to cook until the mushrooms begin to brown just slightly.

5. Raise the heat to high and pour in the beer. Sprinkle with the nutmeg.

6. When the mixture comes to a medium boil, put all the chicken (skin side up, to keep it crispy) and about three-quarters of the bacon back into the pan, reserving the rest of the bacon to finish the dish.

7. Lower the heat to medium-low. Simmer, uncovered, until the chicken is cooked through and the sauce has reduced, about 45 minutes.

8. Remove the chicken from the pan.

9. Add the cream, stirring constantly until warm, and boil until the sauce is somewhat thickened.

10. Return the chicken to the sauce. Taste and adjust the seasoning, if necessary.

11. Add the parsley, sprinkle with the reserved bacon, and serve.

Serves: 2 to 4

INGREDIENTS

3 slices thick-cut bacon, chopped into ¼-inch pieces

4 chicken thighs, bone in and skin on

Coarse sea salt and freshly ground black pepper

1 medium onion, chopped

2 large carrots, halved lengthwise and chopped into ½-inch pieces

2 garlic cloves, thinly sliced

8 ounces button mushrooms, wiped clean and quartered

2 cups lager beer

½ teaspoon grated nutmeg

⅔ cup heavy cream

2 tablespoons roughly chopped fresh parsley

Tipsy Tip

Swap out the lager here for a darker beer as the weather turns from hot to cool. Use whatever beer speaks to the season, to keep it fresh and inspired.

Rob Roy Braised Short Ribs

Serves: 4

INGREDIENTS

6 thick-cut beef short ribs

Coarse sea salt plus freshly ground black pepper

Vegetable oil (optional)

1 red onion, chopped (½-inch pieces, 1 cup)

½ cup chopped carrot (½-inch pieces)

½ cup chopped celery (½-inch pieces)

4 garlic cloves, minced (2 tablespoons)

1 tablespoon tomato paste

1 cup beef stock (page 224)

One 28-ounce can diced tomatoes

6 tablespoons balsamic vinegar

3 tablespoons lightly packed light or dark brown sugar

2 bay leaves

¼ cup decent-quality blended scotch

¼ cup sweet vermouth

1 batch Classic Polenta (page 230)

The Rob Roy is basically a Manhattan but with scotch instead of bourbon. I rarely suggest going sans bourbon, but for this dish, I'll make an exception. Because I know a good drink when I taste one.

And these short ribs are that good drink, but better. Because tender, fall-off-the-bone short ribs elevate anything. Even cocktails. This dish is almost an ethereal experience. I'm warning you, though: you may find yourself groaning with pleasure upon first bite.

INSTRUCTIONS

1. Place a large Dutch oven or deep, oven-safe frying pan over medium-high heat. As it heats, pat the short ribs dry with paper towels and season generously with salt and pepper on all sides. Once the pan is hot, add the ribs and brown all over to develop deep flavor, 3 to 4 minutes per side. Remove from the pan and set aside. Be careful not to overcrowd the pan or you'll steam the meat, rather than sear it. If you must, brown in batches. Once all the meat is browned, set it aside.

2. If much fat hasn't melted into the pan, drizzle with a teaspoon or two of oil. Toss the red onion, carrot, and celery into the pan. Cook until the veggies just start to get a bit of caramelization on them.

3. Add the garlic, stirring constantly for 1 minute.

4. Preheat your oven to 300°F.

5. Add the tomato paste to the veggie mixture, stirring constantly for 2 minutes.

6. When the paste just starts to stick to the bottom of the pan, pour in the beef stock, tomatoes, and vinegar. Stir in the brown sugar and bay leaves and add the browned meat to the mixture. Bring to a boil.

7. Cover and place the pan in the hot oven and braise for 3 hours.

8. After the mixture has braised, remove from the oven and carefully strain the liquid into a medium pot. Set aside to cool slightly and skim the top of any fat that settles there.

9. As it cools, use two forks to pick out the meat from the rest of the solids and shred. Discard the veggies.

10. Make the Classic Polenta.

11. Once you've skimmed the top of the sauce, place the pot over medium-high heat. Add the scotch and vermouth along with the shredded meat. Bring to a boil, lower the heat to medium-low, and simmer until reduced by half. You'll end up with a silky, thick, delicious braised meat sauce.

12. Serve with Classic Polenta and lots of booze.

Tipsy Tip

I've often made these ribs with whatever booze I've had on hand. Anything warm but not too sweet will work—bourbon, brandy, scotch, red wine, port, or even apple cider.

I didn't exactly fall in love with fish the first time I ate it.

This could have been because I was raised inland without a natural lake in sight (how fresh could the catch-of-the-day really be?), or it could have been that I just needed time. And wine. And to come at it at my own pace.

Story of my life.

Since spending the better part of a decade in the Pacific Northwest, fresh seafood has found a major place at my table. I serve fish or some variation of seafood at least a couple times a week, though often more.

A bowl of fresh mussels doused with Gewürztraminer and red Thai chiles (page 131). A parchment parcel of seasonal halibut splashed with grappa, juicy lemon, and Moroccan olives (page 127). Smoked trout piled high with an herby yogurt sauce just slathered on bread like all hell is breaking lose (page 143). Those are my kind of swimmers.

fish & seafood

Parchment-Baked Grappa Halibut
"Cocktail" 127

Dry Vermouth Drunken Clams 128

Gewürztraminer Thai Mussels 131

Sake to Me Scallops 133

Martini Puttanesca & Seared Salmon 136

One Tequila, Two Tequila, Three Tequila,
Ceviche! 139

Ale-Battered Fish (No Chips) 140

Smoked Trout & Brandy Melt 143

Sparkling Panzanella Tuna Niçoise 144

Chardonnay Cazuelitas de Bacalao 147

Parchment-Baked Grappa Halibut "Cocktail"

I use the word *cocktail* loosely here and slightly tongue in cheek. Clearly this isn't a drink.

What it is, though, is a mixture of diverse elements and ingredients—a sum greater than the whole of its parts. And it's got alcohol. And like any good cocktail, it's fresh, well balanced, and made to order.

This is an ode to summer on the West Coast, a tribute to the cocktail, and more important, delicious in your face.

INSTRUCTIONS

1. Remove the fish from the fridge 20 minutes before you're ready to begin cooking. This will help it cook more evenly in the oven.

2. Preheat your oven to 400°F and tear four 12-inch pieces of parchment paper.

3. Place four slices of lemon toward one long end of each piece of parchment. Position the fish on top. Combine the remaining ingredients, except the basil, and season generously with salt and pepper. Pour juice evenly over each fillet.

4. Carefully fold the empty end of the parchment over the fish, lining up one long edge over the other. Fold the sides of the parchment 1/4 inch at a time and then finish by rolling the long edges in the same way. Essentially you're creating a pocket to lock in the juices and steam. Place the wrapped fish on a rimmed baking sheet to catch any drips, just in case.

5. Bake for 15 to 17 minutes, until the fish is cooked through.

6. Remove from the oven and carefully cut a line down the center of each parchment package—be careful of the steam! Garnish with the basil and serve alongside some crusty bread, to soak up the juices, and a fresh salad. Enjoy.

Serves: 4

INGREDIENTS

Four 5-ounce fillets fresh halibut

2 lemons, thinly sliced

2 shallots, thinly sliced (1/3 cup)

2 garlic cloves, thinly sliced

1 tablespoon capers, rinsed

1/4 cup black Moroccan olives, pitted and roughly torn

1/3 cup chopped fresh chives

20 cherry tomatoes, if possible with the vine still attached

20 small asparagus spears, woody ends trimmed

2 tablespoons unsalted butter

3/4 cup grappa

Coarse sea salt and freshly ground black pepper

To garnish: 8 large leaves fresh basil, chiffonaded

Tipsy Tip

You can buy varying thicknesses of parchment paper. Look for brown/darker parchment to wrap up these guys so when you serve them tableside, the paper doesn't break under the weight of the ingredients.

Dry Vermouth Drunken Clams

INGREDIENTS

24 fresh littleneck or Manila clams, purged of sand if necessary (see Note)

1 tablespoon olive oil

1 medium shallot, finely chopped (¼ cup)

1 garlic clove, thinly sliced

Coarse sea salt

¾ cup dry vermouth

1 bay leaf

1 teaspoon dried red pepper flakes

¾ cup fresh oregano leaves

2 tablespoons unsalted butter

To serve: crusty bread or al dente spaghetti, freshly ground black pepper, and lemon wedges

Tipsy Tip

Dry vermouth is a lightly fortified white wine, made with various herbs, spices, and other botanicals and lasts for 2 to 3 months in the fridge. With those things in mind, if you don't have vermouth (though you really should—hello, gin martinis), substitute a floral white wine or even an artisan gin in this recipe.

Most of the dishes I create take a bit of time to come together because I believe in real ingredients—and most real meals take time to prepare. This is not one of those meals.

The great thing about fresh clams is that they cook so dang quickly and often pair with whatever ingredients you have in your pantry, making it easy—and oh so tempting—to enjoy a dish on the patio, on a weeknight, with a cocktail or three in hand.

INSTRUCTIONS

1. When you get them home, keep the clams wrapped (to protect them from cold shock) and on ice (to keep them fresh) in the fridge until you're ready to use them that same day.

2. Place a large saucepan over medium heat with 1 tablespoon of oil. When shimmering hot (but not smoking), add the shallots and a pinch of salt. Stirring regularly, cook until soft and just slightly beginning to color, about 4 minutes. Add the garlic and sauté for another minute.

3. Add the vermouth, bay leaf, oregano, red pepper flakes, and a pinch of salt and bring to a boil.

4. Add the clams and cover. Shaking regularly, cook until all clams are open, about 6 minutes.

5. Mix in the butter. Taste the liquid. Add another pinch of salt, if necessary.

6. Serve with crusty bread or al dente spaghetti to soak up the sauce, plus lots of fresh ground black pepper and lemon wedges.

Note

Ninety-nine percent of the time, you don't need to clean your clams—these days, most good seafood purveyors will do it before they're even sold.

Gewürztraminer Thai Mussels

There's something supremely satisfying—and almost indulgent—about a big pot of fresh shellfish, such as these bivalves, and a bottle of wine. A big steaming bowl of seafood just beckons celebration. Holidays or otherwise. Contentment. Gratitude. Hunger. These are the things I feel when I sit down to a meal like this. Winter, spring, summer, and fall, this is the kind of food worth rejoicing over.

Serves: 2

INGREDIENTS

2 cups cauliflower florets (1-inch pieces)

Virgin olive oil

Coarse sea salt & freshly ground black pepper

2 shallots, thinly sliced (⅓ cup)

1 large garlic clove, minced

2 cups stemmed and roughly chopped Swiss chard

One 1.75-ounce packet yellow curry paste

1 cup coconut milk

½ cup fish stock

½ cup Gewürztraminer wine

¾ teaspoon saffron threads

24 mussels, debearded (see Note)

1 tablespoon chopped scallions

1 bird's eye chile, seeded and sliced

To serve: fresh bread and lime wedges

INSTRUCTIONS

1. Preheat your oven to 450°F and grab a shallow, rimmed baking pan. Toss the cauliflower florets with enough of the oil to coat and a generous seasoning of salt and black pepper. Place in the hot oven and roast until caramelized and tender, 20 to 25 minutes. Remove from the oven and set aside.

2. As the cauliflower roasts, make the rest of your dish! Drizzle 1 tablespoon of oil into a large pot over medium heat. When the oil is hot, toss in the shallots. Stir well and cook until softened, about 3 minutes.

3. Add the garlic. Stirring constantly, sauté for 1 minute.

4. Mix in the Swiss chard and allow to cook until tender, about 3 minutes. Transfer the contents of the pan to a cutting board or small bowl and set aside, returning the pot to the stovetop.

5. Drizzle 1 tablespoon of oil into the hot pan and scrape in the curry paste. Stir constantly over medium heat, until the paste starts to brown slightly.

6. Return the chard mixture to the pan and add the coconut milk, fish stock, Gewürztraminer, saffron threads, and a generous seasoning of salt. Stir to combine and bring to a boil.

7. Add the cleaned mussels to the pot, ensuring they get into the sauce as much as possible. Cover. Cook for 4 for 5 minutes, until the shells open.

8. Remove from the heat and discard any mussels that haven't opened, because it means they were dead long before you got them—don't want you eating any of those.

continued

Farmed mussels are typically a good choice when it comes to inhaling seafood—just make sure they're "off-bottom culture" and not dredged from the seabed. Look for shellfish that are kept in salt water (not fresh—that will kill them) and don't smell like anything at all. When it comes to seafood, fresh is best.

9. Mix in the roasted cauliflower and top with scallions and as much of the chile as you can stand. Be careful—bird's eyes are hot! Serve with lots of bread to sop up the sauce, a bunch of fresh lime wedges, and a bowl to catch the shells as you discard them.

Note

When it comes to mussels, you'll want to make sure you debeard any that have seaweed stuck to them before you cook them. Simply grab the seaweed between two fingers and give it a good tug. It should dislodge fairly easily. Do not soak or rinse under tap water! These are saltwater animals and they are alive—fresh water will kill them, and if they're dead, you can't eat them.

To store uncooked mussels, place in a tea towel over ice in the fridge until ready to cook them later that day; you want them to stay as cold as possible until they're ready to be prepared. Cooked mussels can be eaten for up to 2 days.

Sake to Me Scallops

Scallops are something many of us order in a restaurant but never think to cook for ourselves. But, trust me, these are as simple as they are elegant. The key is to get a really good sear on each side. The scallops themselves cook in about 5 minutes, so you're really just developing the flavors of the sauce to dunk your bread in. The only challenge will be putting down your fork long enough to do so.

INSTRUCTIONS

1. Drizzle 2 tablespoons of the oil into a medium saucepan over medium heat. When the oil is hot but not smoking, add the shallot, garlic, ginger, half of the chile, and the lemongrass. Sauté for 3 minutes.

2. Pour in the sake, lime juice, and fish sauce. Bring to a boil, lower the heat to medium-low, and simmer until the mixture has reduced by half, about 20 minutes. Strain the solids from the sauce. Return the liquid to the pot and stir in the butter. Keep warm until ready to serve.

3. Drizzle the remaining tablespoon of oil into a frying pan over medium-high heat. Pull the scallops from the fridge and remove the muscle on the side of each scallop. This is a slightly different colored skin tag that secures the scallop to the shell. It will feel a bit tough and its fibers run opposite the rest of the scallop. Just pinch it with your thumb and index finger and pull it away. They're edible, so no big deal if you miss one—they're just a little tough to chew.

4. Pat the scallops dry with paper towels and sprinkle generously on all sides with salt and black pepper.

5. When the oil is good and hot but not smoking, add the scallops to the pan. Be careful not to crowd them, or you won't get the beautiful golden sear on them because they'll steam, rather than sear. Do them in batches, if need be.

6. Cook the scallops for 2 to 3 minutes, or until they release from the pan, and flip. Cook for an additional 2 to 3 minutes. Do not overcook, or you'll end up with a rubbery meal.

Serves: 2

INGREDIENTS

3 tablespoons vegetable oil

1 large shallot, sliced (⅓ cup)

2 garlic cloves, sliced

1 tablespoon peeled and grated fresh ginger

1 bird's eye chile, seeded and sliced

1 lemongrass stalk, outer leaves discarded and the remaining stalk bashed a few times with the back end of a knife and then cut into 1-inch pieces

2 cups sake

1 tablespoon lime juice

½ teaspoon fish sauce

2 teaspoons unsalted butter

12 large diver scallops

Coarse sea salt and freshly ground black pepper

1 teaspoon chopped scallions

To serve: crusty bread and lemon or lime wedges

continued

7. Pour the warm sauce into a shallow bowl and place the cooked scallops within it. Garnish with scallions and remaining chile. Serve immediately with crusty bread and lemon or lime wedges.

Tipsy Tip

Sake is Japanese alcohol distilled from grains of rice. The fermentation process is similar to that of beer and, just as for beer, there are varying qualities of sake. This is a bit reductionist, but it'll get you started: Junmai grade is the holy grail, while Honjozo, Daiginjo, or Ginjo grades are also excellent. Some Futsu-shu sakes are good, though they're the equivalent of table wine to most of us and also account for most of the available sake.

Martini Puttanesca & Seared Salmon

Serves: 2

INGREDIENTS

½ cup dried green or brown lentils

1 bay leaf

1 tablespoon virgin olive oil

1 yellow onion, diced (1 cup)

1 tablespoon capers, rinsed

⅓ cup black Moroccan olives, pitted and chpped

2 preserved lemons, flesh discarded, finely chopped

2 garlic cloves, minced

2 teaspoons red pepper flakes

1 cup canned tomatoes, diced

¾ cup good-quality gin

¼ cup dry vermouth

1 tablespoon lemon juice

Coarse sea salt and freshly ground black pepper

⅓ cup roughly chopped fresh flat-leaf parsley

1 tablespoon vegetable oil

Two 6-ounce fillets salmon, deboned

Lemon wedges

This dish was inspired by a staff meal I'd order during a summer waiting tables at a five-star, world-renowned fine-dining restaurant on Galiano Island. Don't be afraid of the number of ingredients—this Moroccan-influenced dish comes together in just over half an hour and is one of the few in the book that's both gluten-free and dairy-free.

INSTRUCTIONS

1. Place 2½ cups water, lentils, and bay leaf in a medium pot over medium-high heat. Bring to a light boil, lower the heat to a simmer, and allow the lentils to cook through, about 30 minutes, adding more boiling water if necessary. You should see just a few bubbles coming to the top to ensure they don't go mushy. Refrain from adding salt until they're finished, or they'll remain crunchy. When four or five lentils are cooked through (no crunch but still intact), drain of any remaining liquid and discard the bay leaf.

2. When 10 minutes are left on the lentils, drizzle the olive oil into a large frying pan over medium heat. When the oil is hot but not smoking, add the onion, capers, olives, and preserved lemons. Stirring often, cook until the onion is just beginning to caramelize.

3. Add the garlic and red pepper flakes, and continue to sauté for 2 more minutes.

4. Stir in tomatoes, gin, vermouth, and lemon juice. Lower the heat and simmer for 4 minutes.

5. Add the cooked lentils, taste, and add salt and black pepper, if necessary. Remove from the heat and stir in the parsley.

6. As the vegetables and lentils cook, fry your fish. Drizzle the vegetable oil into a medium frying pan over medium heat. Pat dry the fish fillets, using a paper towel, and season generously on both sides with salt and black pepper. Place the salmon, skin side down, in the hot pan. Cook for 4 to 5 minutes, until the skin is crispy, then turn and cook for a further 3 to 4 minutes. Remove from the heat and let rest for 3 minutes before serving on the lentils. Garnish with fresh lemon wedges.

One Tequila, Two Tequila, Three Tequila, Ceviche!

If fish could be eaten like a tequila shot—straight down the hatch—it would be in the form of ceviche. Whenever I think of ceviche and/or tequila, my mind sails to my holidays to Mazatlán. To this day, the smells and flavors haunt me like a sexy dream. . . . You just want to fall back to sleep and get it on. Barry White style. So, to satisfy that urge, there's One Tequila, Two Tequila, Three Tequila, Ceviche! And it tastes like Mexico.

Serves: 2 to 4

INSTRUCTIONS

1. To prepare the fish, remove the bloodline (if it exists), and ensure all pin bones have been removed as well as the skin. Chop into ½-inch cubes.

2. Mix the fish with the lime juice, ¼ cup of the tequila, and a pinch of salt. Let sit in the fridge for 20 to 30 minutes, stirring every 10 minutes to ensure an even marinade.

3. Once the fish is opaque, drain most of the lime juice from the bowl, leaving a couple of tablespoons. Mix the remaining ingredients with the fish, adding black pepper to taste. Taste and adjust the seasoning, if necessary.

4. Eat right away and serve with extra lime wedges, tortilla chips, and more tequila. Obviously.

Tipsy Tip

Make sure you use ultrafresh fish for this recipe, because there is no heat to kill off bacteria. Instead, the fish is cured in a bath of citrus juice, which tastes delightful!

INGREDIENTS

1 pound firm white fish e.g., seabass, halibut, sole, cod, or snapper)

⅔ cup lime juice (from about 5 juicy limes)

½ cup reposado tequila

Coarse sea salt

½ small red onion, finely diced (⅓ cup)

1 cup diced cherry tomatoes

1 bird's eye chile, or jalapeño or serrano pepper, seeded and finely chopped

¼ cup finely chopped fresh cilantro

¼ cup black Moroccan olives, pitted and chopped

½ teaspoon dried oregano

¼ teaspoon sugar

½ teaspoon extra-virgin olive oil

Freshly ground black pepper

To serve: extra lime wedges and tortilla chips

Ale-Battered Fish (No Chips)

Serves: 4

INGREDIENTS

1 cup all-purpose flour, plus more for dredging

½ cup cornstarch

12 ounces amber ale beer

Coarse sea salt

Vegetable oil for frying

1½ pounds firm white fish fillets (e.g., cod, haddock, or halibut)

Freshly ground black pepper

To serve: lemon wedges, tartar sauce, and malt vinegar

Tipsy Tip

When deep-frying anything, but especially when deep-frying something coated with batter, make sure your oil is to temperature. If the oil isn't hot enough, the fish won't crisp up and you'll be left with soggy, greasy, soft batter. If it's too hot, you could burn down the house or end up with burned, bitter food. So, just keep an eye on it.

The best fish and chips I ever had was in Paignton, England. It was chucking down with rain, as it's known to do in Britain, so we carted our fish from the chippy and sought refuge under an overhang of a local pub. I ordered us a couple of pints, parked myself to look out at the sea and discovered the fish was wrapped up in real newspaper and the fries were fried so many times they were practically shatterproof. We ate our fish, beachside, under the lip of an otherwise deserted pub, on a very wet day, in the south of England.

INSTRUCTIONS

1. Whisk together the all-purpose flour, cornstarch, amber ale, and 1½ teaspoons of salt in a large bowl. Make sure there are no lumps, but don't overwork the batter. Place in the fridge for 15 minutes.

2. Pour the vegetable oil no more than one-third full into a deep wok or large, heavy-based pot. Heat over medium until it reaches 350°F, or until a 1-inch piece of bread dropped into the oil browns in about 30 seconds. If it browns faster than that, turn down your heat—oil can combust if too hot, and you don't want to break out the fire extinguisher! If it takes longer, then the oil hasn't come to temperature yet.

3. As the oil heats, place a wire rack over a rimmed baking sheet and pour the dredging flour into a medium bowl.

4. Pull the fish from the fridge and pat dry with a paper towel. Season generously on both sides with salt and pepper.

5. When you're ready to fry, pull the batter from the fridge and set close to the oil. Using tongs, dredge the fish in the flour and then submerge in the beer batter. Shake off the excess and carefully lower the battered fish into the oil, ensuring you don't splatter oil or burn your little fingers. Fry for 5 to 7 minutes (depending on the size of your fish), until golden and crispy.

6. Remove the cooked fish from the oil with a large slotted spoon or spider skimmer. Place on the wire rack to drain and season lightly with salt while still hot. Serve with lemon wedges, tartar sauce, and malt vinegar. Eat!

Smoked Trout & Brandy Melt

Even if you don't like fish, you'll probably like this trout. This recipe is meant to be a riff on the classic lox on a cream cheese bagel. The beauty of this sammy isn't just that it's robustly suited for a hefty brunch or lunch or light dinner. It's in the smoky fish–dill yogurt sauce combo, yo. And yum. The more the better! It also just so happens that it makes for great potluck food, too. Gorgeous enough for guests, but takes almost no time or effort to make. Fool them with your brilliance—fool them all. Mwah-ah-ah-ah-ah.

Serves: 4

INGREDIENTS

One 10-inch baguette

2 tablespoons olive oil

½ small red onion, diced (⅓ cup)

1 garlic clove, minced

10 ounces smoked trout (smoked salmon also works well), skin and bones removed

½ cup brandy

6 thin slices Gruyère

1 Batch Herby Yogurt Sauce (page 226)

To garnish: extra dill fronds, roughly chopped

INSTRUCTIONS

1. Preheat your broiler to 450°F and line a shallow baking sheet with tinfoil or parchment paper. Slice the baguette in half lengthwise to separate the top half from the bottom half. Lay, cut side up, on the prepared baking sheet and brush lightly with 1 tablespoon of the oil, to help with browning.

2. Drizzle the remaining tablespoon of oil into a cast-iron pan over medium heat. When hot but not smoking, add the onion. Stir often until just starting to show a bit of caramelization.

3. Toss in the garlic. Stir constantly for 1 minute to make sure it doesn't burn. Garlic can go from yummy to yucky really quickly, so watch it.

4. Add the smoked fish and stir well, breaking up as you go. After about a minute or two, the fish should start to stick to the pan.

5. Carefully pour in the brandy (don't inhale too deeply or you'll get a brandy facial—yikes) and get all the bits up off the bottom of the pan. Allow to reduce until the moisture cooks away, stirring often.

6. Remove from the heat and let cool for 5 minutes. As it cools, place the prepared baguette under the broiler to toast the bread. When golden, 2 to 3 minutes, remove from the broiler.

7. Spoon a generous amount of the Herby Yogurt Sauce on the base of each baguette half. Gently pile the smoked fish on top. Cover with three slices of Gruyère per side—you'll be left with little gaps between the cheese slices. That's okay—that's where you'll cut the sandwiches.

8. Place back under the broiler for a minute or so, until the cheese melts.

9. Remove from the broiler, slice between the cheese segments, and serve! I like to garnish the tops with extra dill fronds and more sauce. Because delicious. Enjoy!

Tipsy Tip

If you have your own smoker, go ahead and smoke your own fish! The freshness of the smoke will only enhance the finished dish. I don't because I live in a tiny apartment in the middle of Vancouver. So, I go to my local fishmonger and get the smoked fish there.

Sparkling Panzanella Tuna Niçoise

Serves: 2 (meal) or 4 (appetizer)

INGREDIENTS

4 large eggs

1 cup halved new potatoes

Coarse sea salt

1 cup green beans, trimmed

⅓ cup plus 1 tablespoon extra-virgin olive oil

¼ cup dry sparkling wine

1 tablespoon Dijon mustard

1 small shallot, finely chopped

1 garlic clove, minced

3 tablespoons lemon juice

2 teaspoons organic honey

Freshly ground black pepper

One baguette

⅓ cup black oily olives, pitted and torn in half

½ cup cherry tomatoes, halved

4 cups roughly torn butter or Bibb lettuce

½ cup fresh basil, torn

1 tablespoon roughly chopped flat-leaf parsley

¼ cup finely chopped fresh chives

4 radishes, thinly sliced

8 ounces sashimi-grade tuna

There are a lot of ingredients in this herbaceous recipe—kind of the opposite of how I tend to cook. I haven't actually created a recipe with this many ingredients since I first started my food blog back in 2010, when I'd throw everything in the pantry, fridge, and cellar into a pot. I'd have included the kitchen sink, too, but I couldn't get the damn thing off the counter.

Don't worry—you've got this like I've got a mason jar of sparkling wine in my right hand. It's really rather simple and just involves some prep time. It's well worth it! Use a crispy, thin French baguette if you can find one.

INSTRUCTIONS

1. Place a large pot filled with water over high heat and bring to a boil. Add the eggs. Boil for 6 to 7 minutes. Remove from the water with a slotted spoon and run under cold water for 1 minute. Peel, slice in half from top to bottom, and set in a bowl. Place in the fridge to chill completely before using.

2. Return the water to a boil and gently add the potatoes to the hot water. Cook for 10 minutes, or until fork-tender. Strain and set in the fridge to chill completely before using.

3. Refill the pot with water and bring to a boil again. Add 1 tablespoon of salt to the water, followed by the green beans. Cook until just fork-tender, 3 to 4 minutes. As they cook, dump a tray of ice cubes into a bowl and cover with cold water. Once the beans are done, strain and immediately place in the ice bath. This will keep them crisp and maintain their brilliant green color. Let chill completely before using.

4. Combine the ⅓ cup of the extra-virgin olive oil, and the wine, mustard, shallot, garlic, lemon juice, honey, and a generous pinch each of salt and pepper in a mason jar. Cover and shake to combine. Taste and adjust seasoning, if necessary. Set aside. The dressing will make more than one salad's worth and will keep up to 1 week in the fridge.

5. Once all your ingredients are cooked and chilled, you can start making your salad! Preheat your broiler to HIGH. Slice the baguette lengthwise to separate the top half from the bottom half. Place, cut side up, on a shallow baking sheet and gently brush with the

continued

To save time the day of: the eggs, potatoes, and green beans (steps 1 to 3) can all be made up to 2 days in advance, while the salad dressing (step 4) can be made up to a week beforehand. If desired, you can serve bread on the side or chop it up smaller to make homemade croutons!

prepared dressing. Broil until golden and crispy, 3 to 5 minutes. Remove from the broiler, cut each half into quarters, and set aside.

6. Drizzle the remaining tablespoon of extra-virgin olive oil into a cast-iron pan over medium-high heat. Pull the tuna out of the fridge and generously season on all sides with salt and pepper. When the oil is hot but not smoking, gently place the tuna in the pan and sear for 30 seconds on all sides. There should be a ring around the outside of the fish that's cooked, while the interior remains raw. Transfer to a cutting board. Allow to cool while you toss the salad.

7. Combine the eggs, baby potatoes, green beans, black olives, tomatoes, lettuce, basil, parsley, chives, radishes, and a generous pinch each of salt and pepper in a large mixing bowl. Add 3 tablespoons of the dressing. You want to taste the dressing but not drench the salad. Mix gently and well.

8. Using a very sharp knife, slice the tuna across the bias into ¼-inch slices.

9. Dish up! Each salad should have a toasted bread base, followed by a nice giant handful of the salad, and then be topped with three or four slices of tuna. Don't worry about its falling off—this is fancy food made messy!

Chardonnay Cazuelitas de Bacalao

Cooking with alcohol doesn't have to mean heavy, wine-laden, cheesy foods. But this particular recipe calls exactly for both of those things. Thank you, Basque Country.

Bacalao is Spanish for "cod." This recipe calls for salt cod, which involves leaching out the salt for 24 hours before cooking with the fish. Of course, even though you pull the salt out, the curing of the fish has had an effect on the texture and flavor of the meat.

The result is tender, flaky, moist, rich, and kind of super delicious. Especially with the combination of the crunchy Parmesan topping with the soft, spreadable texture of the filling.

INSTRUCTIONS

1. Fill a bowl with cold water. Add the fish. Cover. Refrigerate. Change the water two or three times over the next 24 hours, as this will pull the excess salt out of the fish. Drain when ready to use.

2. When the fish has been desalted, fill a small pot with cold water and bring the potatoes to a boil. Cook until tender, 12 to 15 minutes. Drain well and mash with a fork. Put the lid on the pot to keep the potatoes warm.

3. Meanwhile, as the potatoes boil, place the salt cod in another pot of cold water, bring to a boil, then turn off the heat and let the fish sit in there to steep for about 5 minutes. This will allow the fish to cook and become flaky. Then, remove the cod from the hot water and flake with a fork. Make sure there are no bones or skin left in the fish. Place the flaked fish in a food processor. Set aside.

4. Preheat your broiler to HIGH and place an oven-safe bowl on a shallow baking pan.

5. In two shallow pans, separately heat the oil in one and the cream and chardonnay in the other over medium-low heat. Add the garlic to the creamy wine. You want both pans to be very warm but not boiling.

6. With the food processor motor running, slowly and alternately add the warm oil and creamy, boozy garlic mixture to the fish. It should end up looking very gloopy.

continued

Serves: 4 to 6

INGREDIENTS

1 pound salt cod or salt pollock

1⅓ cups peeled and chopped white potato (½-inch pieces; about 1 large potato)

½ cup heavy cream

½ cup unoaked chardonnay

½ cup extra-virgin olive oil

4 garlic cloves, minced

Juice of 1 lemon

⅛ teaspoon grated nutmeg

Coarse sea salt and freshly ground black pepper

¼ cup freshly grated Parmesan cheese

To serve: crusty bread, crackers, or polenta chips

To garnish: sliced radishes and watercress or sprouts

7. Spoon the fish mixture into the potatoes and gently stir to combine, along with the lemon juice, nutmeg, salt, and pepper. Spoon into the oven-safe bowl on the shallow baking dish.

8. Top with the grated Parmesan.

9. Broil until the top is golden and bubbly.

10. Serve with some crusty bread, crackers, or polenta chips, or spread on toasted bread then top with sliced radishes and watercress or sprouts.

Tipsy Tip

When buying salt cod, look to your local fishmonger or Portuguese, Caribbean, or Italian grocer. If you have trouble finding it, substitute salt pollock.

I love getting fresh.

Farm-fresh food. Seasonal drinks. Both at the same time.

Now, that's my kind of night.

The vegetable recipes I've created here are meant to be eaten seasonally and with great gusto. Kind of like cooking with cocktails—it's all in good fun.

It isn't often that veggies are the superheroes of our supper table. When I'm visiting my mom in the Okanagan Valley in British Columbia and ask, "What's for dinner?" she usually replies with one of two answers.

Either "You tell me" or "Hamburgers."

Okay, it might not be hamburgers, but usually the meal is defined by the protein—the star.

Well, my friends, I'm a big fan of the underdog. Those who come from behind and become the unlikely hero.

Like the Watchmen. Or the Guardians of the Galaxy. Or Ricky Gervais.

Or vegetables.

Even if plant-based dishes aren't your favorite food, I can say with slurred confidence that when you quench them in alcohol, you'll like these indulgent veggie-friendly recipes.

Plus, you know, they're served up with bread, cheese, and pasta.

So, if you're into bread, the Margherita "Margarita" Pizza (page 155) should suit you just fine. Or if you're a cheese monkey, try the St. Rita Quesadillas (page 163). Or if you're more of a pasta-kinda-pal, the JD Mac & Peas (page 153) will blow your pasta-lovin' mind.

Or if you simply love a good plate of vegetables as I do, then make them all. Because the only thing better than an underdog story, is an underdog love story.

(mostly) vegetables

JD Mac & Peas   153

Margherita "Margarita" Pizza   155

Mezcal Pan Asparagus & Perfect Poached Eggs   159

Ale Stacked Mushrooms   160

St. Rita Quesadillas   163

Mom's Stout Baked Beans   164

Grappa Ricotta Gnocchi with Bitter Wilted Greens   166

IPA Curried Barley Vegeta-bowls   168

Sauvignon Blanc Brussels Sprout & Mushroom Risotto   171

Cachaça Grilled Avocado with Cachaça Condiments   174

JD Mac & Peas

My JD Mac & Peas is inspired by my friend Julie who loves carbs, Guinness, bourbon, whiskey, cheese, and chocolate chip cookies. She also blogs at *Bread Booze Bacon*. It's loaded with everything that's going to increase your pants size and I want you to enjoy it! In fact, I had one friend love it so much she asked whether I could sell an "onion caramelizing in bacon fat and Jack Daniel's"-scented candle with the book. You know, like the little miniature bottles of alcohol that often come on bigger ones?

Yeah. That would be the dream.

INSTRUCTIONS

1. Line a plate with a paper towel. Place a large, nonstick pan over medium heat, and when hot, add the bacon. Cook until crispy, 13 to 15 minutes. Remove with a slotted spoon and spread over the lined plate, leaving 2 to 3 tablespoons of fat in the pan.

2. Toss the diced onion into the pan of reserved bacon fat and stir well. Cook until the onion gets a decent amount of color (a.k.a. caramelization). Add the garlic. Cook, stirring constantly, for 1 minute longer, or until fragrant.

3. Pour in the Jack Daniel's to deglaze the pan. Bring to a simmer and allow the liquid to reduce to about ⅓ cup. Spoon the entire mixture into a bowl and set aside.

4. As the JD reduces, place a large pot of water over high heat. Bring to a boil, salt generously, and add the macaroni pasta. Stir. Cook until just al dente, 7 to 8 minutes. Remove from the heat, drain, and set aside.

5. Place the butter in the same pot. When it's sizzling and melty, mix in the flour. Continue to cook, stirring, for 2 minutes, or until the mixture becomes dark blond and pastelike.

6. Remove the pan from the heat and pour in the warm milk and smoked paprika, stirring constantly. Place back on the heat element and keep the mixture moving until it thickens and begins to bubble, this should only take a few minutes.

Serves: 6

INGREDIENTS

6 slices thick-cut bacon, sliced widthwise into ½-inch pieces

1 large sweet onion, diced

2 garlic cloves, minced

1 cup Jack Daniel's Tennessee Whiskey

Coarse sea salt

8 ounces dried macaroni pasta

2½ tablespoons unsalted butter

2 tablespoons all-purpose flour

2 cups 2% milk, warmed but not hot, about 98°F (a microwave is good for this!)

2 teaspoons smoked paprika

1½ cups grated Gruyère

1½ cups grated extra-aged Cheddar

1½ cups frozen peas

Freshly ground black pepper

continued

Definitely make this recipe with fresh garden peas when the spring season calls for it! Instead of microwaving them, boil them on the stovetop. Bring a small pot of water to a boil and dump in the fresh peas. Cook for about 3 minutes, or until tender. Wait to add any salt until the peas have finished cooking, though, or they'll get tough. Drain and mix the cooked peas into the saucy pasta.

7. Once the sauce thickens, add the cheeses, one heaping handful at a time, until they melt, mixing well after each addition.

8. Place the peas in a glass bowl with 1 tablespoon of water and, if desired, a dab of butter. Cover and microwave on HIGH for 4 minutes, stirring after 3 minutes.

9. Pour the peas into the cheese sauce along with the Jack Daniel's mixture and cooked pasta. Stir until all the pasta is generously coated.

10. Season to taste with salt and pepper and top with the crispy bacon. Enjoy!

Margherita "Margarita" Pizza

When broaching the "problem" of including a pizza in the book, it only made perfect sense that I make a margarita base for a margherita pizza. Arguably the best pizza. And if it wasn't before, it is now. Even on the days when I'm so exhausted I can't fathom sautéing onions or mushrooms for a topping, this pizza is so good—so simple—I don't mind making the dough.

Serves: 2 to 4

INGREDIENTS

1 packet active dry yeast (about 1 tablespoon)

1 teaspoon sugar

1½ cups plus ⅓ cup warm water

3 cups all-purpose flour, plus more for dusting

Coarse sea salt

Extra-virgin olive oil

Freshly ground black pepper

1 cup fresh basil leaves

1 ball fresh mozzarella, drained and broken into 1-inch pieces

1 batch Margarita Tomato Sauce (page 231)

To serve: 2 limes, cut into wedges

INSTRUCTIONS

1. Place the yeast, sugar, and ⅓ cup of warm water in a bowl. Cover and let sit 10 minutes, or until frothy.

2. Combine the flour and 1 teaspoon of salt in a bowl. Pour the frothy yeast mixture into the flour along with 1 cup of the warm water and mix with your hands to form a dough. Depending on your humidity levels and flour, you may need to add the remaining ½ cup of water: if your dough is too tough, add ¼ cup at a time until it becomes malleable. You want it to be loose enough that you can stretch and shape it, but not so wet that it sticks to your hands uncontrollably.

3. Dust the counter with additional flour and turn out your dough onto it. Knead for 10 minutes, or until smooth and elastic. Add more flour to the counter or your hands, if necessary.

4. Return the dough to the flour bowl along with 1 teaspoon of the oil. Swirl to coat. Cover with a clean dishtowel and set in a warm place for 2 hours to let rise.

5. As the dough rises, make the Margarita Tomato Sauce.

6. Once the dough has risen, punch it down to release the air, cover it again, and let rise 1 more hour. This step isn't fundamental to the recipe, but it increases the flavor in the bread.

7. Once the bread has risen again, preheat your oven to 500°F with two shallow-rimmed baking sheets inside. Let them sit in there for a good 10 minutes at this temperature as it will help the crust become crispy.

continued

Prepare two batches of crust at a time—you'll need to double the ingredients here to do so. After the dough rises, divide and place on parchment-lined baking sheets in the freezer. When frozen, wrap tightly with plastic wrap, label, and then use within six months. This makes Friday night pizza a cinch—just remove from the freezer, place in a bowl in a warm spot in your kitchen, and when you get home from work, it's ready to roll. Literally.

8. Make sure your counter has a good dusting of flour on it. Dump the risen dough onto the flour and cut in half. Roll each piece out ¼-inch thick.

9. Remove the pans from the oven and dust each with flour. Carefully slide the rolled dough onto the hot pans. If this is proving difficult, cut the dough in half or even into quarters (this will make them easier to handle) and make mini pizzas!

10. Pour the sauce over the dough and smooth over the entire surface. Place the pizzas in the oven and bake for 10 to 12 minutes, until just starting to brown on the edges.

11. Remove from the oven and top with the basil leaves and fresh mozzarella. Place back in the oven for a further 5 to 6 minutes, until the cheese is melty and the crust is crispy.

12. Remove from the oven and let it rest for 3 minutes before cutting and serving with lime wedges. Enjoy!

Mezcal Pan Asparagus & Perfect Poached Eggs

Is it just me or does putting an egg on pretty much anything make it better? I'd be tempted to say it's the new bacon; it almost seems like cheating. But you'll love the freshness of the asparagus in this dish, the smokiness of the mezcal, and the saltiness that comes from the pancetta and Parmesan. Combined with the rich yolk of a couple of farm-fresh eggs and you have a seasonal breakfast, lunch, or dinner that any (urban) farmer would be proud to raise.

INSTRUCTIONS

1. Crack the eggs into individual dishes—this will help them keep their shape when you poach them.

2. Bring a large pot of water and the vinegar (helps eggs hold their shape) to a gentle boil over medium-high heat.

3. Add the eggs to the vinegar water, lower the heat to medium, and poach for 4 minutes, or until the whites set but the yolk remains soft. Transfer with a slotted spoon to a plate and sprinkle with salt.

4. Meanwhile, place a large, nonstick frying pan over medium heat. Once it's hot, add the diced pancetta. Cook, stirring often, until crispy, about 5 minutes. It shouldn't be quite as crisp as crispy bacon because it'll crisp up further once you let it cool. Remove from the pan with a slotted spoon and set aside. Pour any remaining grease into a metal container to discard safely when cool.

5. Add the mezcal to the pan. Be careful—it'll splatter. Bring to a simmer and add the asparagus. Boil until the asparagus is just fork-tender. Drain the pan. Place back over the heat and toss the asparagus back in along with the cooked pancetta and lime juice to heat through.

6. Dump the lot onto a serving board and top with the Parmesan and a generous sprinkling of salt and pepper.

7. Place the poached eggs on top and serve!

Serves: 2

INGREDIENTS

4 large eggs

2 tablespoons white wine vinegar

Coarse sea salt

2 ¼-inch medallions of pancetta, diced into ¼-inch cubes

½ cup mezcal

2 pounds asparagus, woody ends snapped off

1 tablespoon lime juice

⅓ cup finely grated Parmesan

Freshly ground black pepper

Tipsy Tip

If you can't find pancetta, prosciutto could be subbed here. Try to get it cut from the butcher directly though so you can order it ¼-inch diced rather than thinly sliced (the way most packaged prosciutto is sold).

Ale Stacked Mushrooms

Serves: 2 to 4

INGREDIENTS

4 tablespoons extra-virgin olive oil

1 pound button mushrooms, wiped with a damp cloth and quartered into 1-inch pieces

Coarse sea salt

4 portobello mushrooms, wiped with a damp cloth and stemmed

Freshly ground black pepper

1 cup amber ale

3 tablespoons unsalted butter

3 cups arugula

½ cup crumbled soft goat cheese

Optional: Madeira Wine Balsamic Reduction and coarse bread crumbs

Tipsy Tip

Although I used less expensive portobello and button mushrooms for this recipe, you can use any edible variety! Let your preferences and nature guide you. Just remember that more delicate mushrooms will require less cooking time.

I've always wanted to go foraging for mushrooms—living in Vancouver, there's ample opportunity. But the risk of paralysis and an agonizing death on the forest floor from eating misidentified ones keeps me in line at the farmers' market. Plus the city just issued in a new law allowing local breweries to sell their ales at the market, so, yeah—literally every single ingredient here can be bought, and relished, locally and in season.

Now, that's the kind of dinner I like to eat. But to be fair, I like to eat all dinners. So, yeah . . .

INSTRUCTIONS

1. Drizzle 2 tablespoons of the oil into a large frying pan over medium heat. When hot, add the button mushrooms. Season well with salt. Sauté until cooked through and golden, about 20 minutes.

2. As they cook, preheat your oven to 400°F. Divide the remaining 2 tablespoons of oil among the portobello mushrooms and rub each with oil on both sides. Season well with salt and pepper. Place in a rimmed baking dish, gills down. Bake for 10 minutes, flip the portobellos, and bake for a further 5 to 7 minutes, until tender. Remove from the oven and set aside.

3. Add the amber ale and butter to the sautéed button mushrooms. Raise the heat to medium-high and poach the mushrooms until the liquid has mostly dissipated and mushrooms are fragrant. Taste and adjust the seasoning, if necessary.

4. Remove from the heat and toss with the arugula, half of the goat cheese, and a pinch each of salt and pepper.

5. To serve, place a portobello mushroom on a plate and gently stack a big handful of the button mushroom mixture on top. Crumble the remaining goat cheese on top of the stacks, and if using, finish with the Madeira Wine Balsamic Reduction (page 221) and coarse bread crumbs.

St. Rita Quesadillas

Inspired by a bottle of St-Germain, these St. Rita Quesadillas have a curious and intriguing sweet note to the savory, and are Mexican-inspired comfort food at its best. Served with my Fiesta Boozy Guac, you may even do a little happy dance while you eat them. If you do, be sure to record it and send me the video. I wanna *see* that shit!

Oh, and be sure to scrape up any crunchy bits of cheese that melt onto the pan—those are a cheesy treat.

INSTRUCTIONS

1. Drizzle 2 tablespoons of the oil into a large frying pan over medium heat. When hot, add the mushrooms and season generously with salt and black pepper. Sauté until the mushrooms are cooked through and starting to get a good amount of color on them.

2. Add the diced onion to the pan and cook for about 5 minutes, or until softened.

3. Toss in the black beans, garlic, cumin, tequila, and St-Germain. Cook for 5 minutes, stirring often.

4. Add the corn and heat through for 1 minute.

5. Pour the stuffing mixture into a bowl, wipe out the pan, and place it back on the heat.

6. Brush one side of one tortilla with a small amount of the oil. Gently set the tortilla in the pan, oil side down, and cover the tortilla with about ¾ cup of the grated cheese and ½ cup of the filling mixture. Sprinkle with a few slices of jalapeño, depending on how spicy you like your food, followed by about another ¼ cup of the cheese. This will help hold the filling in place. Fold the empty half of the tortilla over the filling, using a spatula. When the bottom gets crispy and the cheese starts to get nice and melty, carefully—but swiftly—flip over the quesadilla to crisp the other side. Remove from the pan and set aside on a cutting board. Repeat until all your quesadillas are made.

7. Once the quesadillas are finished, prepare the Fiesta Boozy Guac.

8. Cut the quesadillas into quarters and serve sprinkled with the crumbled feta and remaining jalapeños, with the guac on the side.

Serves: 4

INGREDIENTS

Extra-virgin olive oil

1 pound button mushrooms, wiped clean and quartered

Coarse sea salt and freshly ground black pepper

½ cup peeled and finely diced yellow onion

One 14-ounce can black beans, drained and rinsed

1 garlic clove, minced

½ teaspoon ground cumin

2 tablespoons silver tequila

2 tablespoons St-Germain liqueur

½ cup corn (cooked fresh or drained canned)

1 jalapeño pepper, thinly sliced

4 medium flour tortillas

4 cups grated smoked cheese (Gouda or Cheddar)

½ cup crumbled feta

1 batch Fiesta Boozy Guac (page 232)

Tipsy Tip

St-Germain, a liqueur infused with elderflowers, is highly coveted by cocktail enthusiasts everywhere. It's floral, sweet, and tropical with notes of pear and lychee.

Mom's Stout Baked Beans

Serves: 8

INGREDIENTS

2 ½ cups dried white beans, rinsed and checked for debris

12 cups water

2 teaspoons dry mustard

2 teaspoons coarse sea salt

1 teaspoon freshly ground black pepper

1 yellow onion, sliced

¼ cup lightly packed light brown sugar

½ cup light molasses

5 slices thick-cut bacon, chopped into ½-inch pieces

2 cups stout beer

Tipsy Tip

This recipe makes a substantial pot of beans. Once cooked, freeze half and use within 6 months for a quick—and deliciously boozy—dinner idea.

My mom makes the best baked beans. And homemade buns. Typically, if she makes one, I demand, err, politely request the other. Here, I've introduced stout beer to my mom's recipe. Because when life gives you beans, get beer. Right?

INSTRUCTIONS

1. You don't have to soak your dried beans overnight for this recipe! Place them and 6 cups of the water in a large, oven-safe pot and bring to a rapid boil over high heat. Boil for 2 minute. Remove from the heat, cover, and let soak for 1 hour.

2. Drain the beans and replace the soak water with 6 cups of fresh water. Add the mustard, salt, and pepper. Bring to a boil again and then lower the heat to low, cover, and simmer for 1 hour.

3. Preheat your oven to 300°F.

4. Add the onion, brown sugar, molasses, half of the bacon, and the stout beer. Mix well and return to a boil.

5. Remove from the heat as soon as it starts to boil and sprinkle the remaining bacon on top.

6. Cover the pot and bake for 4 to 5 hours. Remove the lid for the last half-hour to thoroughly brown the pork and create additional flavor.

7. Remove from the oven and serve on toast or with homemade buns or warm naan bread.

Grappa Ricotta Gnocchi with Bitter Wilted Greens

Serves: 4

INGREDIENTS

1½ cups all-purpose flour, plus more for dusting

One 16-ounce container ricotta, well drained (about 1¼ cups)

⅓ cup plus 3 tablespoons grappa

1 large egg

1 large egg yolk

½ cup finely grated Parmesan

Zest of lemon

Coarse sea salt

Extra-virgin olive oil

1 large shallot, thinly sliced (¼ cup)

1 garlic clove, thinly sliced

4 cups bitter greens, rinsed and roughly chopped (dandelion greens, kale, Swiss chard, beet greens, etc.)

⅓ cup golden raisins

1 tablespoon lemon juice

1 tablespoon unsalted butter

Freshly ground black pepper

Gnocchi is one of the first "foreign" foods that changed my life. While I was growing up, there were a lot of meat and potatoes but not much in the way of cultural dishes beyond the scope of Ireland. Imagine my surprise when I grew up, moved out, got taken to a fancy Italian restaurant, and discovered I could still have my potatoes but in dumpling form! Mind. Blown.

Since then, I've created endless reincarnations of gnocchi. I created this dish with my fiancé in mind; he loves bitter flavors. If you aren't huge on bitter, add some fresh steamed or sautéed peas to the wilted greens at the end—they sweeten the dish right up. Or substitute white wine for the grappa.

INSTRUCTIONS

1. Line a baking sheet with parchment paper and a light dusting of flour. Set aside.

2. Place the flour, drained ricotta, 3 tablespoons of the grappa, the egg and yolk, Parmesan, lemon zest, and pinch of salt in a bowl. Mix with a fork until mostly combined and then dump the lot onto a floured countertop and work with your hands until it forms a dough ball. Be careful not to overhandle it, or your gnocchi could become tough.

3. Break off a handful of the dough at a time and roll on the floured surface to form a 1-inch-thick log. Cut the log into ¾-inch pieces and place on the prepared baking sheet. At this point you can cook the gnocchi immediately, place in the fridge for a few hours, or freeze on the baking sheet for use within 1 month. If freezing, let them freeze completely on the baking sheet before you store them in an airtight container. Cook from frozen.

4. Bring a large pot of salted water to a light boil. Gently add 8 to 12 gnocchi to the pot. The gnocchi will be cooked through about 1 minute after they float to the top. Remove with a slotted spoon and set aside until all gnocchi are done.

5. As the gnocchi cook, pour a glug of the oil into a large sauté pan over medium heat. When hot, add the shallot and garlic. Cook for about 2 minutes, or until softened and fragrant.

6. Add the greens, raisins, and lemon juice to the pan. Stir well. Cover. Cook for 4 minutes, or until the greens are wilted and tender. Add the remaining ⅓ cup of grappa, cooked gnocchi, and butter. Allow the moisture to cook away. Season with salt and pepper to taste. Serve immediately.

Tipsy Tip

Because ricotta varies so much in water content, and altitude can affect moisture levels, you may need to play with the flour-to-ricotta ratio a bit to get the texture just right on these. Like any cooking, the more you do it, the better you'll get a feel for it.

IPA Curried Barley Vegeta-bowls

Serves: 4

INGREDIENTS

½ cup plus 2 tablespoons
  extra-virgin olive oil

½ yellow onion, diced
  (½ cup)

1 tablespoon curry powder

1 garlic clove, minced

1 cup pearl barley

22 ounces IPA beer

⅓ cup raisins

2 cups peeled and diced
  sweet potatoes (about 1
  medium)

2 cups small cauliflower
  florets (about 1 medium)

2 cups peeled and diced red
  beets, (about 3 large)

1 tablespoon finely chopped
  fresh rosemary leaves

3 garlic cloves, peeled and
  smashed flat with the
  back of a knife

Coarse sea salt and freshly
  ground black pepper

6 cups stemmed and
  roughly chopped kale

4 large eggs

1 tablespoon white wine
  vinegar, white vinegar, or
  cider vinegar

This is one of those clean-out-the-fridge or use-up-your-CSA kind of dishes. It's a bit thrown together and that's the whole point, so substitute other vegetables according to season or what's in your crisper. It's the kind of fare that warrants a little creativity based on what's in the fridge. Of course, that sometimes requires some ingenuity in cooking methods—some vegetables will need longer or different cooking times than others do, but it's so much fun to see how it all comes together.

INSTRUCTIONS

1. Preheat your oven to 450°F.

2. Drizzle 1 tablespoon of the oil into a medium pot over medium heat. When hot, add the onion and curry powder. Cook until fragrant and the onion has softened, about 5 minutes. Add the garlic and stir constantly for 1 minute.

3. Remove the mixture from the pot, rinse it out, and cook the barley according to the package directions, replacing ½ cup of the recommended cooking water with IPA beer. Watch the pot!—when it starts to boil, it will froth; don't let it boil over. Just remove from the heat for a couple seconds, if need be, it should be good after that. When you add the barley into the pot, also dump in the raisins and reintroduce the curried onion mixture.

4. Place the sweet potatoes and cauliflower in one baking pan and the beets in another. Add ¼ cup of the oil to each pan. Add 3 tablespoons of beer to the yam pan and 2 tablespoons of beer to the beet pan. Add the rosemary to the yam pan and the garlic cloves to the beet pan. Generously sprinkle both with salt and pepper. Toss each pan well to coat. Place in the oven and roast for 20 to 30 minutes, until fork-tender. The yams and cauliflower will likely cook slightly faster than the beets. You won't get a ton of color on the veggies because of their moisture content, but that's okay—the beer will flavor them.

5. While the vegetables roast, cook the kale: Pour the remaining tablespoon of oil in a large, heavy-based pot over medium-low heat. When hot but not smoking, add the kale, ¼ cup of the IPA beer, and a generous pinch of salt and pepper. Stirring often, cook until the kale is wilted down and the liquid is gone. Remove the kale from the pot and set aside.

continued

This recipe makes it really easy to make way too many vegetables and have them on hand for breakfast scrambles for the rest of the week. I'll often double any vegetable I'm roasting, so I can toss them into eggs on gym days or spread them on pizza for dinner.

6. Fill that same pot with water, add the vinegar (helps eggs hold their shape) and place over high heat. Just before the water comes to a simmer, crack the eggs into individual dishes—this also helps them keep their shape. When simmering (but not boiling), lower the heat to medium, and add the eggs. Poach for 4 minutes, or until the whites set but the yolks remain soft. Transfer with a slotted spoon to a plate and sprinkle with salt.

7. Dish up! Place an equal amount of barley, roasted veggies, and kale into a bowl, arranged by color. Top with a couple of poached eggs. Enjoy!

Sauvignon Blanc Brussels Sprout & Mushroom Risotto

A good friend was once visiting me from out of town and he made me the most amazing mushroom risotto. I distinctly remember how long he took to sweat the onions and mushrooms and how perfectly the rice was cooked—al dente with a soft, creamy sauce. Like all good risottos, it wouldn't stand up if you tried to shape it. Rather, it oozes across the plate, silky and smooth, begging to be spooned right up. Kind of like me after a few too many glasses of wine. Sha-bam!

Like our friendship, this risotto has evolved and stood the test of time. I'm thrilled to be part of his wedding party this year and I'm honored to share what started out as his recipe and has grown into a collaboration.

INSTRUCTIONS

1. Preheat your oven to 425°F.

2. Pour the stock into a large pot over high heat. Bring to a light boil, then lower the heat to low to keep warm.

3. As the stock heats, drizzle 2 tablespoons of the oil into a large non-stick pan over medium-low heat. When the oil is hot but not smoking, add the shallot and garlic to the pan. Sauté for 4 to 5 minutes, until softened.

4. As they soften, toss the Brussels sprouts, the remaining 1 tablespoon of olive oil, and a very generous sprinkling of salt and pepper in a roasting pan. Arrange so the Brussels sprouts are cut-side down. Place in the hot oven and roast for 25 to 35 minutes, until crunchy and caramelized. Remove from the oven and set aside.

5. Meanwhile, raise the heat beneath the shallot mixture to medium and toss in the mushrooms and rosemary. Stirring often, cook through until the mushrooms are tender and just starting to get a bit of caramelization on the outside.

6. Add the rice, stirring constantly until grains become translucent on the outside, about 2 minutes.

7. Add the wine, allowing for absorption by the rice and evaporation of the alcohol.

Serves: 4

INGREDIENTS

6 cups chicken, beef, or vegetable stock (page 224)

3 tablespoons extra-virgin olive oil

2 shallots, thinly sliced (⅓ cup)

2 garlic cloves, thinly sliced

1 pound Brussels sprouts, rinsed, dried, and cut in halves, the yucky outer leaves removed

Coarse sea salt and freshly ground black pepper

3 cups sliced button mushrooms (½-inch pieces)

2 sprigs rosemary

1½ cups uncooked Arborio rice

1 cup sauvignon blanc wine

1 cup freshly grated Parmesan

2 tablespoons unsalted butter

continued

8. Ladle enough stock over the rice to just cover the mixture and let simmer, stirring fairly regularly to avoid burning and encourage creaminess. Continue adding further ladlefuls of stock as it gets absorbed, again only as much as is needed to cover the rice. This will continue for roughly 30 minutes, or until the rice mixture is creamy and has reached the desired texture. You want it to be soft but still hold its shape and not be mushy, a.k.a. al dente.

9. Take the pan off the heat, remove the rosemary sprigs, and fold in the Parmesan, butter, and a good grinding of pepper. Stir well to combine. Taste and add more salt and pepper, if necessary.

10. Plate and top with the finished crispy Brussels sprouts. If desired, drizzle a little really good-quality extra-virgin olive oil or truffle oil over the top of each dish. Enjoy!

Tipsy Tip

When making a "white" vegetable risotto, normally any white wine will do. However, use sauvignon blanc for this particular recipe—the grassy notes in the wine pair phenomenally well with the vegetative flavor of brassicas and the earthy flavor of the mushrooms.

Cachaça Grilled Avocado with Cachaça Condiments

Yield: 8 avocado halves

INGREDIENTS

1 tablespoon cachaça

1 tablespoon lime juice

¼ teaspoon smoked paprika

1 tablespoon extra-virgin olive oil

4 Hass avocados, halved and pitted

Coarse sea salt and freshly ground black pepper

1 batch Cachaça Lime Sauce (page 233)

1 batch Cachaça Salsa Fresca (page 234)

Tipsy Tip

You'll end up with extra Cachaça Lime Sauce from this recipe. Use it on Cuervo & Tecate Pork Carnitas (page 100), Gewürztraminer Thai Mussels (page 131), or even just over cheesy eggs in the morning.

Sometimes I just want to eat avocados for dinner. But mowing down avocado on its own isn't usually considered an adequate meal in and of itself. Fools. And when there's no bread in the house—sacrilege!—the notorious avocado toast isn't always an option. This is my answer to the naysayers and unfortunate saps without bread: Cachaça Grilled Avocado with Cachaça Condiments.

Cachaça (pronounced ka-SHAH-suh) is a Brazilian spirit made from sugarcane juice and tastes similar to a marriage of rum and tequila. If you've ever had a caipirinha at a swim-up tiki bar, then you've probably had cachaça. Enjoy el fresco!

INSTRUCTIONS

1. Prepare the cachaça salsa fresca and cachaça lime sauce; set aside.

2. Preheat your grill to 450°F.

3. As it heats, combine the cachaça, lime juice, smoked paprika, and oil in a third bowl and whisk to combine.

4. Brush the mixture on the inside of the avocados and season well with salt and pepper. Reserve the rest of the oil mixture for serving.

5. Place on the grill and heat through for 2 minutes, or until nice grill marks form on the fruit.

6. To serve, place a grilled avocado on a plate and stack with the salsa fresca. Drizzle with the lime sauce. If desired, lightly brush some pita or naan bread with the remaining oil mixture and heat on the grill for 45 to 60 seconds to serve alongside. Enjoy.

I've hosted a lot of dinner parties in my thirty-six years of being. I also went on a lot of dates before I met Dr. Right. In both cases, by the end of the evening we'd be getting a little messy. A little naughty. And be having a lot of fun.

This chapter is for those of us who appreciate a lot of fun. And a happy ending.

Some of the dishes in this chapter are definitively dessert: Raspberry Vodka Brownies & Ganache (page 203) and the Bourbon-Soaked Cherries Tiramisu (page 190).

While others tempt us into dark and twisty places that don't require adherence to a strict label or category. The Dark and Stormy Kettle Corn (page 183) or Grilled Salted Dulce de Leche Chocolate Kahlúa Coffee Sandwiches (page 207), for instance. Are they sweets? Are they late-night snacks? Stoner food? Who cares—they're decadent and highly addictive.

And still others simply make for a juicy, delicious, hedonistic treat. The Layered Naked Champagne Cake with Buttercream Frosting (page 208) is all kinds of crazy. Or the 3-Way Boozy Ice Cream (page 198) which is a frosty choose-your-own flavorsome adventure—gin & tonic, chocolate mint julep, and pralines, rum & caramel.

The point being, at the end of a meal or the end of a date, it's all about pleasure for everyone involved.

And these just desserts, do just that.

sweets

Apple Cider Pound Cake   179

Fried Beignets with Sambuca Coffee Crème Anglaise   180

Dark and Stormy Kettle Corn   183

Spanish Wine-Poached Pears   186

Classic NY-Style Margarita Cheesecake   188

Bourbon-Soaked Cherries Tiramisu   190

Grandma's Chocolate Chip Amarula Cookies   193

Crispy Crunch Bread Pudding   194

Peach Schnapps Blueberry Crisp   197

3-Way Boozy Ice Cream   198

Raspberry Vodka Brownies & Ganache   203

"Old-Fashioned" Pumpkin Pots de Crème   204

Grilled Salted Dulce de Leche Chocolate Kahlúa Coffee Sandwiches   207

Layered Naked Champagne Cake with Buttercream Frosting   208

How to Build a Wine & Cheese Plate   211

Apple Cider Pound Cake

I don't want to set your expectations too high, but this is literally the best cake I've ever had. It's also super simple to make and just yearns for fall. Which, incidentally, is my favorite season of all. I've also got mad rhyming skills. Clearly. Serve with a glass of dry cider or my Cinnamon Apple Whiskey Sour (page 56).

INSTRUCTIONS

1. Preheat your oven to 325°F and generously grease two 6-inch brioche or Bundt pans (a regular Bundt pan would work, too) with butter. Make sure all the inside surfaces are covered. Dust with ¼ cup of the flour, turn the pans upside down and shake out the excess. Set aside.

2. Combine the flour, salt, baking powder, and spices in a medium bowl.

3. Place the granulated sugar and butter in the bowl of a stand mixer and beat at medium speed until light and fluffy. With the motor running, add the eggs and beat until well combined.

4. Combine the cider and vanilla in a small, nonreactive bowl or glass.

5. Starting and ending with the flour mixture, add the dry ingredients alternately with the cider to the butter mixture and mix until well blended.

6. Gently fold in the apple chunks.

7. Pour into the prepared pans and place on a flat baking sheet to catch any drips. Don't worry—it won't rise significantly. Bake in the hot oven for 80 to 90 minutes, until a knife inserted in the center comes out clean.

8. Remove from the oven and allow to cool for 20 minutes in the pan before carefully turning out the cake onto a wire rack to cool completely.

9. To serve, measure the confectioners' sugar into a fine sieve and gently tap all over the cake, coating in a fine dust. Eat.

Yield: 2 or 3 small Bundt cakes or 1 large one

INGREDIENTS

¾ pound (3 sticks) unsalted butter, at room temperature, plus more for pans

3 cups all-purpose flour, plus ¼ cup for dusting

½ teaspoon salt

½ teaspoon baking powder

1 teaspoon ground cinnamon

1 teaspoon ground ginger

½ teaspoon ground cardamom

½ teaspoon grated nutmeg

⅛ teaspoon ground cloves

3 cups granulated sugar

6 large eggs, at room temperature

1 cup dry apple cider

1 teaspoon pure vanilla extract

2 small Granny Smith apples, cored and chopped into ½-inch chunks

To serve: ¼ cup confectioners' sugar and toasted pecans

Fried Beignets with Sambuca Coffee Crème Anglaise

Yield: 16 beignets

BEIGNETS

1 tablespoon active dry
   yeast

¾ cup warm water

⅓ cup granulated sugar

4 cups all-purpose flour,
   plus more for dusting

½ teaspoon salt

1 large egg, lightly beaten

2 tablespoons unsalted
   butter, at room
   temperature

Olive oil for coating

½ cup confectioners' sugar

Vegetable oil for frying

**SAMBUCA COFFEE
CRÈME ANGLAISE**

1 cup whole milk

3 large egg yolks

⅓ cup granulated sugar

Seeds of 1 vanilla bean

½ cup white sambuca

1 cup very strong coffee

So, this restaurant near me makes the most amazing doughnuts. It also
has the *best* fresh oysters and what I call "big girl" servings of wine.
Meaning 9 ounces, in a rocks glass, filled so high to the brim that you
have to slurp the nectar of the gods before you can even pick up the
glass. Similarly to how you'll want to slurp the sambuca coffee crème
anglaise (inspired by what I've had at the restaurant) that makes up
half of this after-dinner treat.

PREPARE THE BEIGNETS

1. Combine the yeast, warm water, and 1 tablespoon of the granulated
    sugar in a bowl. Cover and set in a warm place for 10 minutes. The
    mixture should be good and frothy. If it isn't, that means your yeast is
    dead; start again with a new packet of yeast.

2. Place the flour, salt, and remaining granulated sugar in a stand mixer
    fitted with the paddle attachment. Mix at medium speed until well
    combined.

3. Add the frothy yeast mixture, egg, and butter and mix until a sticky
    dough forms.

4. Turn it out onto the counter and knead for about 5 minutes, until
    smooth.

5. Lightly grease the inside of the mixing bowl with a bit of olive oil and
    transfer the kneaded dough into it, rotating the bowl to gently coat
    the dough in the oil. Cover and set aside in a warm place for 1 to 2
    hours, until the dough has doubled in size.

6. While the dough rises, make the Sambuca Coffee Crème Anglaise
    (instructions follow).

7. Once the dough has risen, pour the vegetable oil into a deep wok or
    pot over medium heat, filling it no more than one-third full. When the
    oil browns a 1-inch cube of white bread in 30 seconds (a.k.a. 350°F),
    it's ready to fry the beignets. Make sure you watch the oil and don't
    let it get too hot. And as always when frying anything, make sure you
    have a fire extinguisher and baking soda nearby in case anything
    catches fire!

continued

Tipsy Tip

The sauce isn't so much of a dip as a thinner variation of an anglaise, meant to moisten and flavor the beignets. We want to enhance them, not obliterate them.

8. As the oil heats, turn out the dough onto a well-floured surface. Cut in half and roll out each half to ¼-inch thick. Cut out 2-inch squares and gently place in the hot oil with a slotted spoon—be careful not to splash yourself or crowd the pan. Fry for 2 minutes per side, or until golden and crispy.

9. Remove the cooked beignets from the oil and drain on a wire rack placed on a plate or rimmed baking sheet. Gently sprinkle the confectioners' sugar over the doughnuts. Serve while hot.

PREPARE THE SAMBUCA COFFEE CRÈME ANGLAISE

1. Heat the milk in a saucepan over medium heat.

2. Meanwhile, in a bowl, whisk the egg and sugar together until smooth.

3. When small bubbles begin to form in the milk, remove from the heat and slowly add the hot milk to the egg mixture, whisking the eggs constantly. This tempers the eggs slowly so they don't cook as soon as the heat hits them. Once fully combined, pour the mixture back into the pot and place back on the heat.

4. Add the vanilla seeds and sambuca.

5. Cook and stir until the mixture thickens and coats the back of a spoon, about 5 minutes.

6. Add the coffee and heat through.

7. Strain the crème anglaise through a fine-mesh sieve to remove any chunks of egg that might have coagulated.

8. Serve with the beignets. The sauce can be made up to 2 days ahead of time and stored in the refrigerator.

Dark and Stormy Kettle Corn

You guys are going to lose. Your. Mind.

The tricky part of this recipe is moisture content. As with baking, altitude can factor greatly with respect to (a) how much you reduce the sauce, and (b) how fluffy/resilient your popcorn is. Start with the best stovetop popcorn you can find; none of this microwavable bull-shit. And then give it a go! If your popcorn disintegrates as mine did the first few times, no worries. It was a hot, melty mess, but luckily my Instagram community helped me along.

If that happens for you, start again and reduce your sauce further, if need be. Pour slightly less of it on the popped corn. Pour it slower, mixing in between additions. It sounds finicky because it is. But I hope to sweet baby Jesus you try this one, because once you figure out your specific moisture-to-popcorn ratio, this will be your new favorite—and highly addictive—habit. Use my recipe as a starting point and go from there.

FYI: The lime juice and zest really are the secret ingredients here. Don't forget them.

Yield: 5 cups corn

CORN

3 tablespoons high-smoke-point oil (vegetable, coconut, peanut)

⅓ cup popping corn kernels

2 teaspoons kosher salt

SAUCE

1 cup ginger beer

¼ cup dark rum

¼ cup lime juice (from about 2 juicy limes)

4 tablespoons (½ stick) unsalted butter

½ cup light brown sugar

¼ teaspoon baking soda

Zest of 1 lime

PREPARE THE CORN

1. Preheat your oven to 275°F. Line a baking sheet with parchment paper and set aside.

2. Heat the oil, three corn kernels, and 1 teaspoon of salt in a large, covered pot over medium-high heat.

3. When the kernels pop, remove from the heat and add the remaining kernels. Cover immediately and count out loud to 30. This method first heats the oil to the right temperature, then waiting 30 seconds brings all of the other kernels to a near-popping temperature so that when they are put back on the heat, they all pop at about the same time.

4. Crack the lid just a tiny bit to allow steam to escape and return the pot to the heat. As the corn pops, shake the pot every 20 seconds or so to ensure all the kernels make their way to the bottom to pop and nothing burns. When the popping slows to several seconds between pops, dump the popcorn into a large bowl. Set aside. Be sure to wipe out any stuck-on bits of popcorn from the pot with a paper towel, so they don't burn during the sauce-making process.

continued

PREPARE THE SAUCE

1. Pour the ginger beer, rum, and lime juice into the pot. Be careful—it's hot and may spit and sputter! Lower the heat to medium and place back on the burner, bring to a light boil, and simmer until the mixture reduces by two-thirds. Pour into a bowl and set aside.

2. Now add the butter and brown sugar to the pan. Give it a good stir to combine and then allow to melt and bubble at the edges.

3. Lower the heat to medium-low and cook, stirring often, for about 5 minutes, or until thickened, amber in color, and a little bit sticky.

4. Remove from the heat, mix in the reduced alcohol, and add the baking soda, stirring vigorously. You'll want to move quickly here—this is pseudo-candy we're working with and we don't want it to cool.

5. Pour over the popcorn and mix with a spatula to ensure even coating.

6. Spread over the prepared baking sheet as a single layer, sprinkle with the remaining teaspoon of salt, and place in the hot oven. Bake for 40 to 45 minutes, to dry the corn.

7. Remove from the oven, let cool, and then break into clusters. Sprinkle with the lime zest.

8. Try to control yourself. ;)

Tipsy Tips

Serve this popcorn in a copper bowl and with a couple "Moscow" Dark and Stormys (page 36)—they were meant for each other!

Spanish Wine-Poached Pears

Serves: 4 to 6

INGREDIENTS

Juice of 2 lemons

1½ cups Tempranillo wine

1 cup water

2 cinnamon sticks

1 teaspoon whole cloves

1 cup sugar (organic cane sugar or honey would be interesting, too)

¼ teaspoon salt

1 organic lemon, thinly sliced

4 firm but ripe Bartlett pears (Bosc will also work)

To serve: 1 lemon, thinly sliced, and ice cream

Tipsy Tip

Tempranillo as a wine varietal is incredibly food friendly and is priced at an excellent value. Because of the sweetness of the pears, the savory vegetal yet fruity notes of this grape make it an ideal match for this dish.

As one of my good friends who has made this recipe says, "Wine-poached pears are the shit." Truer words have never been spoken. This recipe is oh so easy (kind of like me on the third date) and totally delicious. Who would ever argue with a wine, cheese, and pear course? Or a cheap and easy writer with a saucepan full of wine, for that matter?

Make these pears as the weather turns cooler and as the holidays approach—if they don't purr "cozy," I don't know what does. Serve with a healthy scoop of ice cream. I recommend the freshness of the Gin and Tonic Ice Cream in particular (page 198).

INSTRUCTIONS

1. Place the lemon juice in a shallow bowl. Set aside.

2. Place the wine, water, cinnamon sticks, cloves, sugar, salt, and slices of one lemon in a medium saucepan over medium-low heat and gently allow the sugar to dissolve, stirring often.

3. Once the sugar dissolves, raise the heat to medium-high and bring to a gentle boil. Cook for 15 minutes.

4. Peel and core the pears. You can do this by slicing them in half and removing the pear cores with a paring knife, or if you have a corer, just plunge that baby headfirst into the center of the fruit and pull out the core. As you do this, gently toss the pears in the reserved lemon juice, to prevent browning.

5. Add the pears to the saucepan—this will bring down the temperature of the liquid. Once it starts to boil again, lower the heat to medium and simmer for a further 20 minutes, occasionally turning the pears gently, if necessary, to ensure even coloring.

6. Turn off the heat, cover the pot, and leave the pears to soak in the syrup at least 6 hours (or overnight).

7. Before serving, remove the pears and simmer the syrup over medium-high heat for about 15 minutes, or until it thickens slightly. When there are 5 minutes left on the timer, add the pears back to heat through.

8. Serve the pears with some of the syrup mixture, a slice of fresh lemon, and a scoop of ice cream. Enjoy!

Classic NY-Style Margarita Cheesecake

Serves: 6 to 8

CRUST

3.5 ounces graham crackers

¼ cup sugar

1 teaspoon coarse sea salt

4 tablespoons (½ stick) unsalted butter, melted

FILLING

26.5 ounces full-fat cream cheese, softened

¾ cup sugar

1 cup full-fat sour cream

1 teaspoon pure vanilla extract

Zest and juice of 1 lime

¼ cup tequila

2 tablespoons orange liqueur (Grand Marnier or Triple Sec)

4 large eggs, at room temperature

To garnish: lime wheels

Cheesecake is one of those things where, if it strikes my fancy, it sure as hell had better strike my tongue soon, too. This cheesecake is as light as air in your mouth and decadently creamy. The key is to wipe down the sides of your mixing bowl as you go, so everything gets incorporated, and then add your eggs one at a time to get a ton of air up in that cheesy biznass. Add some tequila and lime to that cake, and you now have one of the greatest inventions of our time (oh yes, I went there): Classic NY-Style Margarita Cheesecake.

PREPARE THE CRUST

1. Preheat your oven to 375°F.

2. Pulse the graham crackers in your food processor until finely ground. Add the remaining ingredients and pulse until combined. Firmly line a 9-inch springform pan with the mixture, going up the sides as high as you can. Make sure the bottom and sides are even and carefully but firmly packed. Place in the oven and bake 12 to 14 minutes, until golden, crisp, and smelling delicious. Remove from the oven, place the pan on a wire rack, and allow to cool completely.

3. Once the crust has cooled, set your oven to 325°F and roll some tinfoil around the bottom of the pan and two-thirds of the way up the sides, to prevent water from leaking into the bottom. Place in a deep roasting pan large enough for the springform pan to sit flat.

PREPARE THE FILLING

1. Place the cream cheese, sugar, sour cream, vanilla, lime zest and juice, tequila, and orange liqueur in the bowl of a stand mixer (alternatively, you may use a large bowl and an electric hand mixer). Beat at medium-high speed until creamy and light, 3 to 4 minutes. Make sure to wipe down the sides as you go, so everything gets creamed together.

2. Beat in the eggs, one at a time, mixing well after each addition.

3. Pour the cream cheese mixture into cooled crust. Fill the roasting pan with boiling water so that it comes halfway up the sides of the springform pan. Carefully place in the oven and bake for 50 to 60 minutes, until the center of the cake still jiggles but the outer inch and a half looks set and cooked through.

4. Turn off the oven and open its door to allow the heat to dissipate slowly. After 45 minutes, pull the cake from the oven and gently lift the pan from the water bath. Run a knife around the outside of the cake to prevent it from sticking and cracking the top.

5. Place on a wire rack to cool completely. Cover and refrigerate for 24 hours. If you can . . . serve garnished with additional lime wheels and a classic margarita!

Tipsy Tip

It's easy to want to dive face-first into a cheesecake the moment it comes out of the oven, but trust me—planning ahead to give it 24 hours to fully set will greatly enhance the texture and experience of the cake.

Bourbon-Soaked Cherries Tiramisu

Serves: 6

INGREDIENTS

1½ cups cold heavy cream

1 teaspoon pure vanilla extract

2 tablespoons confectioners' sugar

2 cups cold, strong brewed coffee

6 tablespoons orange liqueur (e.g., Triple Sec or Grand Marnier)

2 tablespoons Kahlúa

One 14-ounce package ladyfingers

One 8-ounce container mascarpone

3 tablespoons granulated sugar

1 to 2 large handfuls of Bourbon-Soaked Cherries (page 216), pitted and roughly torn

2 ounces dark chocolate, grated

Tipsy Tip

Double the coffee brewed and store the excess in the fridge to easily throw together Dirty Sexy Coffee Drinks (a.k.a. Shafts) (page 47) for guests, should the occasion call for it. Because it usually does.

It's my professional opinion that a good tiramisu should be as caffeinated as it is boozy, as cheesy as it is sweet. My Bourbon-Soaked Cherries Tiramisu is all of those things. You do have to make it ahead of time so the ladyfingers (light, egg-based cakes you find in the cookie aisle at the grocer's) have time to fully expand and incorporate the liquid. I've served this an hour after making it but the additional rest time benefits the overall experience greatly.

So does more bourbon. Or Kahlúa. Or orange liqueur. Take your pick—this dish has all three.

INSTRUCTIONS

1. To make the whipped cream: Pour the cream into the bowl of your stand mixer, fitted with the wire whip attachment. Whip on high speed for 4 to 6 minutes, until soft peaks form. Add the vanilla and confectioners' sugar, folding them in until just combined. Place in the fridge until ready to use. Alternatively, you could use an electric hand mixer and bowl—it just takes longer.

2. Combine the coffee and booze in a bowl.

3. In a larger bowl, whisk together the mascarpone, whipped cream, and granulated sugar.

4. Dip the ladyfingers, one at a time, into the coffee mixture for 3 to 5 seconds each, and lay in the bottom of a glass baking dish or 6 to 8 individual cups.

5. Spread half the cheese concoction over the soaked ladyfingers and top with the cherries, reserving one cherry for the garnish of each serving of tiramisu.

6. Repeat the dipping of ladyfingers, followed by the cheese, and top with whipped cream, grated chocolate, and the cherry garnish. Cover with plastic wrap and refrigerate for 3 to 24 hours.

Grandma's Chocolate Chip Amarula Cookies

These cookies are fluffy, not too sweet, and more than one person who's been on the receiving end of a box of these little morsels have definitively christened them "cake cookies." And they're famously addictive.

Only now they've grow'd up with Amarula cream—a decadent, fruity, slightly nutty liqueur that is worth the purchase. It may even replace Baileys in your Sunday coffee. Gasp!

INSTRUCTIONS

1. In a small bowl, combine the flour, salt, and baking soda. Set aside.

2. In a large bowl, cream the butter and brown sugar together with an electric hand mixer on medium speed until combined and slightly fluffy.

3. Add the eggs and vanilla, mixing until combined.

4. Starting and ending with the flour mixture, add the dry ingredients to the wet mixture in thirds, alternating with the Amarula cream, mixing well to combine after each addition.

5. Fold in the chocolate chips throughout the batter, all the way to the bottom.

6. Cover and place the dough in the fridge for 30 to 60 minutes to chill. This will help ensure the cookies don't spread when they're in the oven.

7. While the dough chills, preheat your oven to 350°F and line two cookie sheets with parchment paper.

8. Grab 2 teaspoons and spoon 1 1/2-inch scoops onto the prepared baking sheets, leaving an inch or two between them to allow room for cookie expansion.

9. Bake for 12 to 15 minutes, until the bottoms are slightly firm and golden brown.

10. Transfer to wire racks to cool (if you can wait!) and then chow down with a big glass of Amarula cream over ice.

Yield: 36 to 40 cookies

INGREDIENTS

3 cups all-purpose flour

1 teaspoon baking soda

1/2 teaspoon fine salt

2 cups lightly packed light or dark brown sugar

1/2 pound (2 sticks) unsalted butter, at room temperature

2 large eggs, lightly beaten

1 teaspoon pure vanilla extract

3/4 cup Amarula cream liqueur

1 1/2 cups semisweet or dark chocolate chips

Tipsy Tip

These babies freeze super well, making them a great treat to keep on hand for company or holidays. Although that won't stop you from sneaking one when no one's looking; I often eat them straight out of the freezer. The way the chocolate chips crunch is just addictive!

Crispy Crunch Bread Pudding

Serves: 6 to 8

BREAD PUDDING

1 cup raisins

½ cup Frangelico

½ cup crème de cacao

1 loaf stale bread, cut
into 1-inch pieces
(about 6 cups)

¾ cup granulated sugar

¾ cup lightly packed dark
brown sugar

2 cups 1% milk

4 large eggs

2 teaspoons pure vanilla
extract

CRUMBLE TOPPING

½ cup lightly packed dark
brown sugar

5 ⅓ tablespoons cold butter,
cut into ½-inch pieces

2 teaspoons ground
cinnamon

To serve: evaporated milk
or ice cream

I generally prefer my desserts more on the savory side. Or in a rocks glass. More often than not I've been known to order a bourbon whiskey with a side of ice for an after-dinner treat. But a Crispy Crunch shot—consisting of half Frangelico, half crème de cacao, shaken and then strained into a glass—is something I can't resist. And as bread pudding, it's damn good.

PREPARE THE BREAD PUDDING

1. Place the raisins, ¼ cup of the Frangelico, and ¼ cup of the crème de cacao in a small bowl, stir, and marinate for 15 minutes. Set aside.

2. As the raisins sit, lightly grease a 9-by-13-inch baking pan and pre-heat your oven to 375°F.

3. Mix together the remaining ¼ cup each of Frangelico and crème de cacao and the granulated sugar, brown sugar, milk, eggs, and vanilla in a large mixing bowl. Sprinkle the raisins over the bread. Incorporate their liquid into the milk mixture and toss with the bread.

4. Pour the whole lot into the prepared baking pan.

PREPARE THE CRUMBLE TOPPING

1. Rinse out the bowl, dry, and combine the crumble topping ingredients. Breaking up the butter with your fingers, sprinkle the mixture over the top of the bread pudding.

2. Place in the oven and bake for 45 minutes, or until the liquid has been absorbed, the top is golden, and the pudding has set.

3. Serve hot, drizzled with evaporated milk or a scoop of ice cream

Tipsy Tip

The idea behind this dessert is that you get to have the soft, yummy bread and the crunchy, buttery topping. I like more of a pop or hint of the topping, but if you want more, you can double the topping ingredients without penance.

Peach Schnapps Blueberry Crisp

Alone, peach schnapps is sickly sweet. Think those five-cent fuzzy peach candies you used to buy from the convenience store. But folded into ripe peaches and gorgeous, fresh blueberries in the height of summer, it sings of sunshine. There's something truly special about a good crisp. The rustic elegance, the pastoral simplicity. Just a bowl of fruit, some oats, and a spoon. And in this case, peach schnapps.

PREPARE THE CRISP

1. Lightly grease a 9-inch square baking dish and preheat your oven to 375°F.

2. Combine the peach schnapps, lemon juice, vanilla, brown sugar, salt, cinnamon, allspice, and cornstarch in a large mixing bowl.

3. Add the fruit and coat well. Pour into the prepared baking dish.

PREPARE THE CRUMBLE

1. In the same bowl, combine all the ingredients for the crumble.

2. When well combined, sprinkle over the top of the filling.

3. Bake in the oven for 35 to 45 minutes, until the top is crisp and golden.

4. Serve topped with a nice big scoop of ice cream. Enjoy!

Tipsy Tip

Use fresh summer fruit for this recipe. While frozen berries and stone fruit can work really well in a smoothie, as a sauce, or part of a reduction, they're far too liquidy for a crisp. With the addition of schnapps, this recipe already creates a fairly loose filling—you don't want fruit soup. Or maybe you do. Your call.

Serves: 6

CRISP

3 cups fresh blueberries

½ cup peach schnapps

1 tablespoon lemon juice

1 teaspoon pure vanilla extract

½ cup dark brown sugar

½ teaspoon salt

1 teaspoon ground cinnamon

1 teaspoon ground allspice

2 tablespoons cornstarch

5 fresh peaches, cored and sliced into ½-inch slices (about 3 cups)

CRUMBLE

2 cups rolled oats

1½ cups dark brown sugar

½ pound (2 sticks) unsalted butter, at room temperature

1 teaspoon ground cinnamon

¼ teaspoon grated nutmeg

Pinch of salt

To serve: ice cream

3-Way Boozy Ice Cream

Serves: 6 to 8

BASE (ALL 3)

1½ cups heavy cream

1½ cups whole milk

5 large egg yolks

½ cup granulated sugar

¼ teaspoon salt

Oh the possibilities of frozen cream and sugar!

The base for all three of these is delicious yet mild enough to take on *any* flavor! If you want to create your own boozy ice cream (and why wouldn't you?), keep in mind that three to four shots of alcohol makes it boozy and delicious. Try five if you want—just make sure your freezer is very cold. More than five and it won't want to freeze because of the alcohol content.

Note: Remember to place your ice-cream attachment and bowl in the freezer at least 24 hours before making ice cream. These instructions are for a KitchenAid stand mixer ice-cream attachment, though if your ice-cream machine differs, that's cool. Use according to your manufacturer's instructions. The recipes will still work.

Also, it is very important to read the directions *all the way through* before beginning, so that your variation ingredients will be ready to add at the right step (6 or 7) of the base recipe instructions.

PREPARE THE BASE

1. Place the heavy cream and milk in a medium pot over medium heat and heat, stirring often. You want the liquid to become quite hot but not boil.

2. As the milk heats, prepare an ice bath. Fill one bowl with ice and lay a second, slightly smaller one inside it. Then place a fine-mesh strainer inside that. Set aside.

3. When the cream is almost ready, whisk the egg yolks, sugar, and salt together in a third bowl until the mixture becomes pale.

4. Slowly ladle 1 cup of the cream mixture into the egg mixture, whisking constantly. This will slowly temper the yolks and prevent you from making scrambled eggs.

5. Slowly pour the creamy egg mixture into the pot of the remaining cream and lower the heat to medium-low.

6. Stir constantly for 10 minutes, or until the mixture thickens and coats the back of a spoon. Be sure to get all the way to the edge of the pot to make sure the custard doesn't burn.

7. Strain the custard through the sieve into the bowl on the water bath, to catch any bits of egg that might have cooked.

continued

GIN & TONIC VARIATION

¼ cup gin

½ cup tonic

2 tablespoons lime juice

To garnish: lime zest

CHOCOLATE MINT JULEP VARIATION

¼ cup bourbon whiskey

1 teaspoon pure peppermint extract

⅓ cup unsweetened cocoa powder

½ cup roughly chopped dark chocolate

To garnish: fresh mint leaves

PRALINES, RUM, & CARAMEL VARIATION

1 batch Dulce de Leche (page 235)

1 cup pecans

½ cup dark brown sugar

1 tablespoon water

½ teaspoon ground cinnamon

⅛ teaspoon coarse sea salt

¼ cup dark or spiced rum

8. You can now leave the custard in the water bath for 30 minutes, stirring often to cool completely, or cover and place in the fridge for 3 to 12 hours.

9. When it's completely cooled, it's time to churn, baby, churn! Remove the ice-cream bowl from the freezer and attach to your stand mixer. Attach the drive assembly and dasher and set the power to STIR.

10. Pour the chilled custard into the ice-cream bowl. Be sure your motor is running when you add the custard, or it could freeze the moment it hits the bowl. Churn for 17 to 20 minutes, until the ice cream becomes a stiff soft-serve consistency.

11. Using a rubber spatula, transfer the ice cream to a freezer-safe container—I like using bread pans! Cover tightly with foil and place in the freezer for 12 to 24 hours, to freeze completely.

PREPARE THE GIN & TONIC VARIATION

1. Once you strain the custard into the ice bath bowl (step 7), add the gin and tonic ingredients.

2. Follow the remaining base recipe to finish the ice cream.

PREPARE THE CHOCOLATE MINT JULEP VARIATION

1. When the custard is hot and before you strain it (steps 6 to 7), add the chocolate mint julep ingredients, except the fresh mint.

2. Whisk over low heat until completely dissolved.

3. Follow the remaining base recipe to finish the ice cream. Sprinkle fresh mint on top when serving.

PREPARE THE PRALINES, RUM, & CARAMEL" VARIATION

1. Preliminarily, make Dulce de Leche. Set aside. Bring to room temperature before using.

2. Make the pralines: Line a baking sheet with parchment paper. Set aside. Place the pecans, brown sugar, water, cinnamon, and salt in a small pot over medium heat. Once the sugar gets bubbly and most of the moisture has cooked away, spoon the candied pecans onto

the prepared baking sheet in one layer. Let cool completely. Roughly chop. Store in an airtight container in the fridge for up to 2 weeks.

3. Once you strain the custard into the ice bath bowl (step 7), add the rum.

4. Continue with the remaining base recipe.

5. When you spoon the churned ice cream into a freezer-safe container (step 10), do so in three layers, sprinkling the pralines and drizzling the *dulce de leche* between the layers.

6. Follow the remaining base recipe to finish the ice cream.

Tipsy Tip

Ice cream will keep a good 2 weeks before developing ice crystals. Remove from the freezer about 5 minutes before serving—homemade ice cream tends to be harder than store-bought and it benefits from a brief respite from the freezer before you gobble/ mow/slurp it up.

Raspberry Vodka Brownies & Ganache

Moist. Rich. The perfect brownie. Need I say more?

Yield: 20 brownies

PREPARE THE BROWNIES

1. Lightly butter a 9-by-13-inch baking pan and preheat your oven to 350°F.

2. Place the butter and semisweet chocolate in a double boiler over medium heat. If you don't have a double boiler (I don't), pour a couple of inches of water in a pot and fit a heatproof bowl over the top. Place the chocolate and butter in the bowl. Stir constantly to avoid burning until the chocolate melts and the butter is well incorporated. Remove from the heat and set aside to cool.

3. In a separate bowl, combine the eggs, sugar, vanilla, and vodka.

4. Thoroughly mix the cocoa powder into the chocolate.

5. Stir the egg mixture into the chocolate cocoa mixture to combine.

6. Fold in the salt and flour until just combined. Do not overmix!

7. Pour into the prepared baking pan. Bake for 35 to 45 minutes, until the brownies are set and slightly pulling away from the pan.

8. Remove from the oven and let cool completely before glazing.

PREPARE THE GANACHE

1. Place the dark chocolate in a small, heatproof bowl; set aside.

2. Slowly heat the cream and vodka in a small saucepan until it just begins to boil. Pour over the chocolate and let stand for about 30 seconds; whisk until the chocolate is melted and the mixture is blended. Add the butter and mix until smooth.

3. Chill briefly until thickened, about 15 minutes.

4. Spread over the cooled brownies. Top with berries and hazelnuts.

5. Refrigerate at least 1 hour to set ganache. Or you know, eat it gooey right away. I did.

BROWNIES

½ pound (2 sticks) unsalted butter, at room temperature, plus more for pan

10 ounces semisweet chocolate

4 large eggs, at room temperature

2 cups sugar

1 tablespoon pure vanilla extract

½ cup raspberry vodka

½ cup unsweetened cocoa powder

1 teaspoon salt

1 cup all-purpose flour

GANACHE

10 ounces dark chocolate, roughly chopped

½ cup heavy cream

2 tablespoons raspberry vodka

1½ tablespoons unsalted butter, at room temperature

To garnish: 1 cup fresh raspberries and 1 cup toasted and roughly chopped hazelnuts

"Old-Fashioned" Pumpkin Pots de Crème

Serves: 6

INGREDIENTS

1 cup heavy cream

¾ cup whole milk

2 tablespoons bourbon whiskey

2 dashes Angostura (or preferred) bitters

⅔ cup pure maple syrup

¾ cup pure pumpkin puree (avoid "pumpkin pie filling")

7 large egg yolks (save the whites for breakfast!)

1 teaspoon pumpkin pie spice

⅛ teaspoon salt

1 batch Bourbon Whipped Cream (page 236)

I have yet to meet a person in my life who doesn't love pumpkin pie. It's like corn (or its boozy subsidiary, bourbon) or Chris Pratt—our body is just hard-wired to want it. Warm spices speak to us of autumn and seasonal celebrations in houses brimming with friends and family. This dessert is an "adulted" ode to those days gone by. Whiskey, maple, and pumpkin were pretty much meant for one another. These are rich, smooth, silky, and reminiscent of pumpkin pie, sans crust. But don't worry—you won't miss it. The Bourbon Whipped Cream more than makes up for the lack of crunch.

INSTRUCTIONS

1. Prepare the Bourbon Whipped Cream; set in the fridge until pots de crème are ready.

2. Place six ungreased oven-safe, individual-size ramekins in a high-rimmed roasting pan and preheat your oven to 325°F.

3. As the oven comes to temperature, combine the cream, milk, bourbon whiskey, bitters, maple syrup, and pumpkin puree in a saucepan. Place over medium heat and bring to a simmer, stirring regularly. Once lightly bubbling, remove from the heat.

4. Whisk the egg yolks, pumpkin pie spice, and salt in a medium bowl.

5. Gently pour just a few drops or so of the hot cream into the eggs, whisking constantly. Once the mixture is warm, very slowly pour the egg mixture into the hot cream, whisking constantly. This slowly tempers the eggs, so they don't cook and become all chunky in the pudding.

6. Divide the crème equally among the ramekins, leaving ¼ inch of headspace at the top.

7. Pull the middle oven rack out of the oven by a few inches and place on it the pumpkin-filled ramekins, in their roasting pan. Fill the roasting pan with hot water (I use a kettle of boiled water for ease) so it reaches halfway up the outside of the ramekins. Carefully slide the rack back into the oven. Bake for 35 to 40 minutes. The top should be set like a pumpkin pie while the centers will still have a bit of jiggle to them.

8. Pull the roasting pan out of the oven. Be careful—that water is hot! Set on a wire rack for 15 minutes to cool slightly. Carefully remove

the ramekins from the hot water bath and place in the refrigerator for 4 to 24 hours, to cool and set completely.

9. Serve with a heaping tablespoon of Bourbon Whipped Cream.

Tipsy Tip

Although canned pumpkin puree is available year-round, when pie pumpkins are in season, you can easily make your own puree. Nothing tastes as good as fresh. Simply slice the pumpkin into quarters, spooning out the innards, and roast in a 350°F oven for 30 to 40 minutes. Scoop the flesh off the skins and puree until smooth. I often make a few pumpkins worth of my own puree in late September/ early October and chuck it in a freezer bag by portion size, label it, and then use it throughout the year.

Grilled Salted Dulce de Leche Chocolate Kahlúa Coffee Sandwiches

This late-night snack is ultra-badass. Totally rockin'. And kinda greasy. It's a funny one and one that will have you coming back for more. It isn't quite dessert; it isn't quite a savory dish. It exists in this strange dark and twisty place I like to call late-night snacks. Like stoner food, it's highly yum, highly unhealthy, and highly addictive. If you can stop yourself from mowing down the *dulce de leche* or chocolate-Kahlùa coffee before it gets on the bread, you're in for a treat!

INSTRUCTIONS

1. Prepare the Dulce de Leche; set aside.

2. Place the coffee, cream, Kahlúa, and chocolate in a double boiler over medium heat. (If you don't have a double boiler—I don't—pour a couple of inches of water in a pot and fit a heatproof bowl over the top. Place the chocolate, coffee, and cream in the bowl.) Stir constantly to avoid burning until the chocolate melts and the coffee and cream are well incorporated. Remove from the heat and set aside. It will thicken and become more spreadable as it cools.

3. Place a cast-iron pan over medium-high heat.

4. As it warms, butter one side of each piece of bread, just like making a grilled cheese sandwich. Place the buttered bread, butter side down, in the pan and cook until toasty and browned.

5. Remove from the pan and slather half of the bread slices with as much caffeinated creamy chocolate as you can stand; do the same with the Dulce de Leche on the remaining slices. Get messy. I like you messy.

6. Sprinkle one side with a pinch of flaky sea salt and marry the two sides. Cut in half. Repeat until all the sandwiches are pieced together.

Yield: 4 sandwiches

INGREDIENTS

3 tablespoons strongly brewed coffee

2 tablespoons heavy cream

3 tablespoons Kahlúa

1 cup (60–70%) dark chocolate chips

1 medium loaf sourdough bread, cut into ½-inch slices

Butter for spreading

1 tablespoon flaky sea salt (e.g., Maldon)

1 batch Dulce de Leche (page 235)

Tipsy Tip

You can make the Dulce de Leche and coffee ahead of time, up to 3 days in advance. To really get crazy, garnish with Bourbon-Soaked Cherries (page 216), fresh summer strawberries, or seasonal winter oranges.

Layered Naked Champagne Cake with Buttercream Frosting

Serves: 8 to 10

CHAMPAGNE CAKE

½ pound (2 sticks) unsalted butter, at room temperature, plus more for pans

3 cups all-purpose flour

1 tablespoon baking powder

1 teaspoon salt

2 cups granulated sugar

7 large egg whites

Seeds of 1 vanilla bean

2 cups dry sparkling wine (e.g., expensive champagne or less expensive Spanish Brut or Cava)

For serving (optional): fresh berries or edible flowers

BUTTERCREAM FROSTING

1 pound (4 sticks) unsalted butter, at room temperature

4 cups confectioners' sugar

1½ teaspoons pure vanilla extract

Don't be scared of the butter. I'll say it again: Don't be scared of the butter.

The best thing about naked cakes (other than the fact that they're cake. And naked.) is that you don't have to be a pastry chef to get the decorating just right. So go ahead—I give you permission to throw the rules out the window and get messy.

The flecks from the vanilla seeds throughout the cake are almost magical and the wine gives it a very French yeasty aroma that I enjoy both in cake and old-world wines. With a moist, tender crumb and a gorgeous chewy, golden outside, this champagne cake is as mouthwatering as it is beautiful.

PREPARE THE CHAMPAGNE CAKE

1. Line three 7-inch springform pans with parchment paper and grease lightly with butter. Preheat your oven to 350°F.

2. Combine the flour, baking powder, and salt in a medium bowl. Mix well. Set aside.

3. In a larger bowl or the bowl of your stand mixer, beat the butter and sugar together at medium speed until light and fluffy.

4. Mix in the vanilla bean seeds and add the egg whites, one at a time, beating well after each addition.

5. Beat in the flour mixture and sparkling wine alternately, starting and ending with the flour mixture. It should go flour, wine, flour, wine, flour. Be sure to scrape down the sides of the bowl as you go, to get everything incorporated.

6. Divide the batter among the prepared pans (2 cups per pan) and gently tap on the counter to remove any air bubbles and flatten the top of the batter—this will help you achieve a flat cake.

7. Bake for 35 to 40 minutes, or until a toothpick inserted into the center comes out clean.

8. Remove the cakes from the oven and let sit for 10 minutes. Remove from the pans and turn onto a wire rack to cool completely before frosting.

Tipsy Tip

Fancy this cake up for tea and coffee with edible flowers and fresh berries or make it super fun for a party with multicolored sprinkles! You can make this cake as fancy pants or casual as you want.

PREPARE THE BUTTERCREAM FROSTING

1. Place the butter in a large bowl or the bowl of a stand mixer. Beat at high speed until the butter is pale and creamy, 2 to 3 minutes. Reduce the speed to medium-low and add the confectioners' sugar, ½ cup at a time, beating well after each addition and scraping down the sides of the bowl as needed. Once each addition of the sugar is incorporated, raise the speed to high for 20 seconds to aerate the frosting. Then lower the speed to medium-low and add the next ½ cup of sugar (or you'll end up with a cloud of sugar. Everywhere.).

2. Once all the sugar is incorporated, leave the speed on high speed, pour in the vanilla, and beat for a further minute.

3. To frost, place a dab of frosting on the serving plate—this will keep the cake in place. Set one layer of the cake on the plate and use an offset spatula (or butter knife) to spread a ¼-inch layer of frosting on the top of the cake. Place the second layer of the cake on top of the whole shebang and repeat the frosting method until all layers are stacked. Then sparingly cover the top and sides of the cake with the remaining frosting. Garnish with fresh berries and/or edible flowers. Don't worry about its looking unfinished or messy—it's supposed to; she's naked!

Note

If you don't have three 7-inch springform pans, you can also use two 9-inch—your cake just won't be as high. Or if you only have one springform pan, divide the batter into three equal portions and bake one at a time. It'll clearly take longer this way, but the batter will wait for you.

The frosting will keep in the fridge for up to 10 days and can be made ahead of time. If stored, bring to room temperature and rewhip for a few minutes before using, to make it easily spreadable and light.

How to Build a Wine & Cheese Plate

This is hardly a recipe. It's more an assemblage directive. Wow—that sounded serious, didn't it? But really, when wine and cheese are concerned, a bit of seriousness is warranted. Until it's served. Then it's time for shit to get cray-zay.

In Europe most cheese courses are served between the main and dessert course or before the main meal, but a cheese plate is by far one of my favorite ways to end one. Whether it be a romantic night in with J, a gathering of friends on *The Walking Dead* night, or just me alone on a Gulf Island writing a book (ahem), cheese + wine = perfection.

The key to assembling a cheese plate is to keep it simple. A small assortment of fresh local cheeses with varying textures (think: hard, soft, and bloomy) and/or origins (cow, sheep, goat), some fruit, maybe a couple complementary accents. That's it.

It sounds simple, but a lot of people mess it up by overcomplicating things, either in the ingredients or in the delivery. To help you along, here is a list of inclusions as well as some basic instructions on how to help make your cheese course the best it can possibly be.

When deciding how much cheese to get, I typically suggest two to four different kinds (see next note), allocating 3 to 4 ounces per person.

When choosing cheese, get a small variety of textures and/or origins so the experience of the board varies and diners can "choose their own adventure" with each bite. I suggest something salty and grainy or crumbly, something soft and creamy, and something semisoft or hard. Or, to keep it simple, one of each main category of cheese: aged, soft, firm, and blue. If all else fails and you aren't sure—ask your cheese monger! Just like farmers at the farmers' market, these guys love to talk shop.

Remember when you're foraging for your cheese board ingredients that the accompaniments should reflect something about the cheese. Going Greek? Grab some olives, sun-dried tomatoes, and dates. Traveling to Italy? Some finely sliced prosciutto, polenta chips, and a red wine fig spread would pair nicely. Making the journey to Spain? A bowl of Marcona almonds, sliced figs, and marinated artichoke hearts would be delicious. Or visiting eastern Europe? How about some grainy mustard and gherkin pickles? If you're going on a world tour, include one element of each.

Don't forget the bread. Whether you make homemade crostini or use boxed crackers, avoid flavored bread—while an integral part of the cheese platter, it's really just a vehicle to get the cheese to the mouth.

Take all the ingredients out of the fridge 1 to 3 hours before serving your cheese course. Not only does cheese "relax" to its intended texture, it also ensures none of the flavors are masked by being too cold.

Slice harder cheeses before you serve them on a separate board than what you're serving on—this will keep the board looking clean in presentation, which should be arranged in a similar fashion as what the brick originally looked like.

Arrange your cheeses clockwise on the board, from mildest to strongest in flavor. This allows guests to experience each cheese and not overwhelm their palate. It also helps people with more sensitive taste buds know what might be too much for them.

Don't crowd the board. If people have to delicately slice, dice, and arrange the platter because it's so full that shit's falling onto the table, they'll feel awkward. If your board is just a little too small for what you're serving, use multiple platters or dishes. And use mismatched ones, to keep it fun! You can use wooden cutting boards, marble tiles, glass cake platters, ceramic pottery, or any other food-grade surface that's flat.

Label the cheese if you can't keep straight what each one is. Score cute labels at any craft store or winery. Include the title of the cheese, the animal it came from, and what country or province. That way guests know what they're eating and learn a little something along the way. And it saves you from having to memorize and recite all that information over and over again, which can be difficult, depending on how much wine you've had.

Use a separate cutting/serving knife for each cheese to preserve the unique flavor profile of each. You can get cheese knife sets at most home goods stores. Worst-case scenario: use any knife in your kitchen. The important thing is that the cheese finds your mouth.

Wine. Obvi. Generally white wine pairs better with a cheese plate and cuts through the richness of it all, but I prefer red. Go with whatever makes your mouth happy.

Have a few Formaticum cheese bags on hand for the end of the night for quick cleanup of leftovers. They allow the cheese to breathe and help regulate humidity. They also make pretty awesome gifts. One of the coolest things I've ever received was a little wax-coated paper bag imprinted with the date, cheese, and animal. Oh yeah, and there was leftover Brie inside.

Most important, eat lots of cheese. Drink too much wine. Enjoy.

I'm a firm believer in keepin' it real. And when you want really good food, it's gotta start from somewhere honest. And in my cooking, that often means an onion, some garlic, and getting a bit handsy.

The tasty-factor of a finished dish is only as good as the ingredients you use. There are places to make exceptions—I don't make my own phyllo pastry, nor do I press my own corn tortillas or age my own cheese. Mainly this is due to time and space constraints. Could you imagine having your own cheese cellar?! #Want.

But there are some staples that I insist on buying premium—extra-virgin olive oil, balsamic vinegar, and tequila. Others, I refuse to do anything but make from scratch, such as BBQ and pizza sauce, salad dressings, and stock. Other ingredients, such tomatoes and strawberries, demand seasonality—because they just taste better that way. Besides, taking the extra time to craft a dish from the ground up gives me an excuse to crack open that bottle of wine eyeing me from across the room.

Making these things at home takes a little more time to prepare than buying the packaged product from the store, but as you'll see, they're usually quite simple and straightforward. They're also ridiculously useful beyond the pages of this book.

For example, you can use the Margarita Pizza Sauce as a base for a bolognese pasta; the Basic Stock as the foundation for any soup, stew, or sauce your pretty little head can come up with; the Spiced Yogurt Sauce as a light lunch paired with some roasted carrots and kale pesto; or the Bourbon Whipped Cream as foreplay.

Hey, man—whatever you choose to do with these staples and sauces is between you and your stockpot.

Point being, these recipes are useful, delicious, and can be applied to multiple recipes that you find both here and in your own kitchen.

staples & sauces

Bourbon-Soaked Cherries   216

Simple Syrup   218

Balsamicy Onions   219

Bloody Mary Tomato Jam   220

Madeira Wine Balsamic Reduction   221

Drunk Pear Salad Dressing   221

Mojito Watermelon Salad Dressing   222

Sparkling Rosé Roquefort Salad Dressing   223

Homemade Stock   224

Spiced Yogurt Sauce   225

Herby Yogurt Sauce   226

Smoky Stout *or* Maple Whiskey BBQ Sauce   227

Quick Pickled Onions   228

Bordelaise Sauce   229

Classic Polenta   230

Margarita Tomato Sauce   231

Fiesta Boozy Guac   232

Mango Salsa   233

Cachaça Lime Sauce   233

Cachaça Salsa Fresca   234

Dulce de Leche   235

Bourbon Whipped Cream   236

Bourbon-Soaked Cherries

These are a treasured and coveted item in my house. Only the closest of friends get a shot at these. I guard them with vigilance.

This recipe makes a limited amount for small-batch canning—something even a novice canner or someone with limited space can do. But the recipe easily bulks up if you want more. I usually can about 100 half-pint jars myself each and every year. And then store them in my cellar, a.k.a. the back of my closet.

For this, you don't have to sterilize the jars, lids, or rims in advance—just make sure they're clean and dry.

When ready to serve, spoon over ice cream, stuff in between cake layers, use in the Bourbon-Soaked Cherries Tiramisu (page 190), or even better—take three and dunk 'em in more bourbon. I regularly plop a couple into a Boulevardier (page 35) or Maple Bacon Bourbon Manhattan (page 51).

Eat. Or drink. Or both.

1. Sit down with a Boulevardier (page 35) or Maple Bacon Bourbon Manhattan (page 51) and pit the cherries. The OXO cherry pitter feels good in your hand and works very well.

2. Place the water and sugar in a medium-sized saucepan. Bring to a light boil, stirring constantly, until the sugar dissolves.

3. Add the lemon juice and vanilla. Remove from the heat.

4. As you dissolve the sugar, you can bring a water-bath canner full of water to a boil. If you have don't have one, just use a very deep, wide stockpot with one of those old-fashioned metal steamers laid out in the bottom. This will keep the jars off the bottom of the pot so they don't break. Fill the pot with water and bring to a rolling boil.

5. Using very clean hands, place the pit-free cherries in the jars, leaving 3/4 inch of headspace at the top of the jars. Pour the sugar syrup over the cherries (still leaving that 3/4 inch of space at the top) and spoon 1 to 2 ounces of bourbon whiskey over the entire mixture, depending on how boozy you like your fruit. This should leave you with 1/2 inch of headspace.

6. Wipe the rim of the jars with a clean, dry towel, and secure the rims and lids. Air needs to escape from the jars when you boil the jars, so tighten the lids just enough that there's no give when you try to tighten further but not so hard that you have to fight to get them open.

7. Place in the boiling water and boil for 15 minutes to ensure seal and sanitization.

8. Carefully remove from the water with a jar lifter (or a pair of tongs with rubber bands wrapped around the ends to prevent slippage) and set on a clean towel. Allow to set for up to 12 hours. You may hear a "ping" noise coming from the jars—this is an excellent sign.

9. Once completely cool, unscrew the rings and check to make sure the lids have in fact sealed and refrigerate any that don't. Although you should use unsealed cherries within a couple of weeks, the sealed ones will last you up to a year. Store the sealed jars in a cool, dark place.

Yield: 4 half-pint jars cherries

INGREDIENTS

4 cups red summer cherries

2 1/2 cups organic cane sugar

2 1/2 cups water

Juice of 1 lemon

1 teaspoon pure vanilla extract

6 to 12 ounces bourbon whiskey

Tipsy Tip

One year I actually used Booker's bourbon for these because it was so boozy on its own it knocked me on my ass. That was an expensive batch of cherries. You don't need to buy super expensive or artisan small-batch bourbon for this recipe. A middle-of-the-road spirit will do. Think Maker's Mark, Bulleit, or similar.

Simple Syrup

Yield: 1 cup syrup

INGREDIENTS

1 cup sugar

1 cup water

INSTRUCTIONS

1. Place the sugar and water in a small saucepan over medium heat. Allow the sugar to dissolve and thicken the liquid, stirring often until it reaches a light boil. Remove from the heat and allow to cool completely before using.

Balsamicy Onions

Yield: 1 cup onions

INGREDIENTS

Extra-virgin olive oil

2 large onions, sliced

2 teaspoons salt

1 cup balsamic vinegar

INSTRUCTIONS

1. Heat a couple glugs of the oil in a large frying pan over medium-low heat.

2. When hot, add the onions and salt, stir well to coat. Cook for 25 to 30 minutes, stirring occasionally.

3. Add the vinegar and allow to reduce until it's thick and coats the onions but not burning in the pan, about 25 minutes.

4. Remove from the heat and let cool.

Note

The balsamicy onions will keep for up to 1 week in the fridge, but are best enjoyed within 5 days.

Bloody Mary Tomato Jam

INGREDIENTS

Extra-virgin olive oil

30 fresh curry leaves

1 teaspoon yellow mustard seeds

½ teaspoon cumin seeds

2 garlic cloves, minced

¾-inch fresh ginger, peeled and finely grated

1 tablespoon tomato paste

1 pint cherry tomatoes, halved

½ cup vodka

Juice of 1 lemon

1 teaspoon grated fresh horseradish

4 dashes Worcestershire sauce

Pinch of sugar

Pinch of salt

INSTRUCTIONS

1. Heat the oil in a medium frying pan over medium heat until hot.

2. Add the curry leaves, mustard seeds, and cumin seeds and sauté until just beginning to "pop."

3. Add the garlic, ginger, and tomato paste and continue to cook for 1 minute, stirring constantly.

4. Add the tomatoes, vodka, lemon juice, horseradish, Worcestershire, sugar, and salt and stir well. Simmer over low heat for 15 to 20 minutes, stirring occasionally, until the tomatoes have softened and the sauce has thickened.

5. Remove from the heat and allow to cool slightly before serving.

Madeira Wine Balsamic Reduction

Yield: 1 cup balsamic reduction

INGREDIENTS

1 cup dry Madeira wine

2 cups balsamic vinegar

1 tablespoon sugar

INSTRUCTIONS

1. Place the wine, vinegar, and sugar in a medium saucepan over medium heat.

2. Bring to a simmer and reduce to 1 cup, or until it's thick enough to coat the back of a spoon.

Note

If it thickens too much as it cools, just add a couple of tablespoons of water and reheat. The reduction will keep for up to 3 weeks in the fridge.

Drunk Pear Salad Dressing

Yield: 1 cup dressing

INGREDIENTS

⅓ cup extra-virgin olive oil

2 tablespoons balsamic vinegar

1 tablespoon lemon juice

1 tablespoon pear liqueur

⅛ teaspoon ground cardamom

Coarse sea salt and freshly ground black pepper

INSTRUCTIONS

1. Place all the ingredients in a mason jar. Cover tightly and shake to combine. Adjust for taste.

Note

The salad dressing will keep for up to 1 week in the fridge. Just remove from the fridge 30 minutes before using, to allow the oil to come to room temperature and emulsify.

Mojito Watermelon Salad Dressing

Yield: ½ cup dressing

Note

The salad dressing will keep for up to 5 days in the fridge. Just remove from the fridge an hour before using, to allow the cheese to come to room temperature and emulsify.

INGREDIENTS

¼ cup white rum

3 tablespoons lime juice

1 teaspoon organic cane sugar

Splash of olive oil

Coarse sea salt and freshly ground black pepper

INSTRUCTIONS

1. Place all the ingredients in a mason jar. Cover tightly and shake to combine. Adjust for taste.

Sparkling Rosé Roquefort Salad Dressing

Yield: 2 cups dressing

INGREDIENTS

½ cup dry sparkling rosé wine

1 cup Roquefort blue cheese

¼ cup sour cream

2 tablespoons buttermilk

2 tablespoons fresh grapefruit juice (from about ½ grapefruit)

1 tablespoon Dijon mustard

1 tablespoon bacon fat

¼ cup fresh chives, finely chopped

Flaky sea salt and freshly ground black pepper

INSTRUCTIONS

1. Place all the ingredients in a food processor or blender.

2. Puree until well combined and smooth.

3. Adjust the seasoning to taste.

Note

The salad dressing will keep for up to 5 days in the fridge. Just remove from the fridge an hour before using, to allow the cheese to come to room temperature and emulsify.

Homemade Stock

Yield: 8 cups stock

Note

The stock will keep for up to a week in the fridge or 6 months in the freezer.

INGREDIENTS

Carcass of 1 chicken, turkey, or rabbit; or beef, veal, or duck bones

10 cups cold water

2 celery stalks, roughly chopped

1 sweet onion, quartered

3 medium carrots, roughly chopped

2 leeks, roughly chopped and tough green tops discarded

5 garlic cloves

Juice and zest of 1 lemon

1 Parmesan rind

Large handful of fresh herbs (e.g., rosemary, thyme, basil, and/or bay leaves)

Coarse sea salt and freshly ground black pepper

INSTRUCTIONS

1. Place all the ingredients in a big-ass pot over high heat. Bring to a simmer, but don't let it boil.

2. Lower the heat to a low simmer, partially covering the pot, and let simmer for 5 to 7 hours, skimming the top as necessary to remove any excess fat.

3. Once the time's up, place a colander over a deep bowl and strain the stock. Be careful—it's hot and you don't want a steam facial. If you pour really slowly and carefully, you will have a clearer stock—I don't care about that, so I just dump it as quickly as possible.

4. Wipe out the pot and strain a second time through a fine sieve from the bowl back into the pot. Taste and adjust the seasoning, if necessary.

5. Place the stock in the fridge to cool for a couple of hours and then scrape any fat off the top.

Spiced Yogurt Sauce

Yield: 1 cup sauce

INGREDIENTS

½ teaspoon coriander seeds

½ teaspoon ground cumin

½ teaspoon ground fennel

½ teaspoon red pepper flakes

½ teaspoon yellow or red curry powder

½ teaspoon smoked paprika

½ teaspoon coarse sea salt

Zest of 1 lemon

1 cup plain full-fat Greek yogurt

INSTRUCTIONS

1. In a mortar and pestle (or spice grinder), crush the spices until fragrant.

2. Grind in the lemon zest.

3. Combine spice mixture with the yogurt in a medium bowl.

4. Place in the fridge until ready to serve.

Note

The spiced yogurt sauce will keep for up to 2 days in the fridge.

Herby Yogurt Sauce

Yield: ¾ cup sauce

INGREDIENTS

½ cup plain, full-fat Greek yogurt

⅓ cup full-fat sour cream

1 tablespoon capers, rinsed

1 tablespoon lemon juice

2 tablespoons finely chopped fresh chives

1½ teaspoons finely chopped fresh dill

Coarse sea salt and freshly ground black pepper

INSTRUCTIONS

1. Combine all the ingredients, including a generous pinch of salt and pepper, in a medium bowl.

2. Taste and adjust the seasoning as necessary.

Smoky Stout *or* Maple Whiskey BBQ Sauce

Yield: 2 cups sauce

INGREDIENTS

2 tablespoons unsalted butter

½ large onion, diced

3 garlic cloves, minced

1 cup stout beer *or* maple rye whiskey (if unavailable, regular rye whiskey and a tablespoon of pure maple syrup will do)

¾ cup ketchup

¼ cup cider vinegar

2 tablespoons adobo sauce (from a can of chipotle peppers in adobo sauce)

¼ cup Worcestershire sauce

2 tablespoons light or dark brown sugar

1 tablespoon smoked paprika

1 teaspoon dry mustard

½ teaspoon ground cumin

INSTRUCTIONS

1. Heat the butter in a medium pot over medium heat. When sizzling and melty, add the onion and garlic. Sauté until soft and fragrant, about 5 minutes.

2. Add the remaining ingredients and bring to a boil. Lower the heat to medium-low and simmer for 20 to 25 minutes, stirring often.

3. Remove from the heat and pour the mixture into a food processor. Puree at high speed until smooth. Alternatively, you can use an immersion blender, but be careful—it's hot!

4. Pour into a mason jar or other nonreactive vessel.

Note

The BBQ sauce will keep for up to 2 weeks in the fridge.

Quick Pickled Onions

Yield: 1 cup onions

Note

The pickled onions will keep in the fridge for up to 1 week.

INGREDIENTS

1 small red onion, sliced into thin rounds (a mandoline is handy for this)

½ cup white wine vinegar

1 tablespoon sugar

1 teaspoon coarse sea salt

INSTRUCTIONS

1. Combine all the ingredients in a nonreactive bowl. Mix well.

2. Let sit to "quick pickle" for at least 45 minutes.

Bordelaise Sauce

Yield: 1 cup sauce

Note

The sauce will keep in the fridge for up to 3 days.

INGREDIENTS

3 sprigs fresh parsley

3 sprigs fresh rosemary

3 sprigs fresh thyme

1 bay leaf

1 cup Bordeaux wine

½ shallot, finely diced

Coarse sea salt and freshly ground pepper

2 cups veal or beef stock (page 224)

2 tablespoons unsalted butter

INSTRUCTIONS

1. Create a little satchel (a.k.a. a bouquet garni) out of cheesecloth around the parsley, rosemary, thyme sprigs, and bay leaf. Knot at the top. Place in a medium saucepan along with the wine, shallot, and a generous helping of salt and pepper. Bring to a light boil over medium heat and allow the liquid to reduce by half.

2. Pour in the veal stock and bring back to a light boil. Reduce the mixture to 1 cup.

3. Stir in the butter and you'll be left with a silky, smooth sauce. Season to taste with salt and pepper and remove the bouquet garni.

Classic Polenta

Serves: 4 to 6

INGREDIENTS

4 cups chicken stock (page 224)

1 cup water

Juice of 1 lemon

1½ cups fine polenta

¾ cup grated Parmesan

2 tablespoons unsalted butter

INSTRUCTIONS

1. Pour the chicken stock, water, and lemon juice into a large saucepan over medium-high heat. Bring to a light boil and lower the heat to medium-low.

2. Pour the polenta into the liquid slowly, to avoid clumping, whisking constantly.

3. Continue to stir for about 10 minutes, until the meal has thickened, cooked through, and is of your desired consistency. If your polenta is quick cooking, it could be ready in as little as 2 to 3 minutes. Taste it if you're unsure. At the last minute, dump in the Parmesan and butter. Stir well to mix through and serve.

Margarita Tomato Sauce

Yield: 2 cups sauce

INGREDIENTS

Extra-virgin olive oil

1 medium yellow onion, diced

Coarse sea salt

2 garlic cloves, minced

One 28-ounce can good-quality tomatoes (e.g., San Marzano)

1 bay leaf

1 teaspoon dried Italian seasoning

1 cup tequila

Freshly ground black pepper

INSTRUCTIONS

1. Heat 1 tablespoon of the oil in a saucepan over medium heat.

2. When hot, add the onion and a pinch of salt and sauté until the onion just starts to brown.

3. Add the garlic and cook for 1 minute, or until fragrant.

4. Add the tomatoes, bay leaf, Italian seasoning, tequila, 1 teaspoon of salt, and a good helping of pepper. Stir well.

5. Bring to a boil and turn the heat to medium-low. Simmer for 40 minutes, or until the mixture reduces and gets thick and pulpy.

6. Remove from the heat and puree until smooth.

Note

The tomato sauce will keep for up to 1 week in the fridge and gets even better the day after cooking.

Fiesta Boozy Guac

Yield: 2 cups guacamole

INGREDIENTS

2 ripe avocados, halved and pitted

½ small red onion, finely diced (⅓ cup)

1 garlic clove, minced

⅓ cup sweet tomatoes, chopped into ½-inch pieces

⅓ cup corn (cooked fresh or drained canned)

¼ teaspoon ground cumin

2 tablespoons lime juice

1 tablespoon silver tequila

1 tablespoon St-Germain liqueur

Coarse sea salt and freshly ground black pepper

Optional: ½ jalapeño pepper, seeded and finely chopped, and/or ¼ cup finely chopped fresh cilantro

INSTRUCTIONS

1. Scoop the avocado into a bowl and mash with a fork until spreadable but still chunky.

2. Add all the other ingredients. Mix well.

3. Taste. Season further with more salt and pepper, if necessary.

4. Note: Serve immediately.

Mango Salsa

Yield: 2 cups salsa

INGREDIENTS

1 ripe mango, peeled, pitted, and diced into ¼-inch cubes

1 avocado, peeled, pitted, and diced into ¼-inch cubes

1 small red bell pepper, seeded and diced into ¼-inch cubes

½ small red onion, finely diced

2 tablespoons lemon juice

¼ cup chiffonaded fresh basil

Coarse sea salt and freshly ground black pepper

INSTRUCTIONS

1. Place all the ingredients, including a generous pinch of salt and pepper, in a bowl. Stir to combine.

2. Season to taste.

Note

The salsa will keep for up to 3 days in the fridge.

Cachaça Lime Sauce

Yield: 1 cup sauce

INGREDIENTS

1 cup crème fraîche

1 tablespoon cachaça

Zest and juice of 1 lime

¼ teaspoon smoked paprika

¼ teaspoon coarse sea salt

INSTRUCTIONS

1. Combine all the ingredients in a bowl. Mix well.

2. Spoon into a squeezable bottle for easy application.

Note

The lime sauce will keep for up to 5 days in the fridge.

Cachaça Salsa Fresca

Yield: 3 cups salsa

Note

The salsa fresca will keep for up to 3 days in the fridge.

INGREDIENTS

2 cup diced cherry tomatoes

2 garlic cloves, minced

½ red onion, finely diced

1 bird's eye chile (a small red one), seeded and finely chopped

¼ cup chopped fresh basil

¼ cup chopped fresh cilantro

1 teaspoon dried oregano

1 tablespoon lime juice

2 teaspoons extra-virgin olive oil

1 teaspoon balsamic vinegar

1 tablespoon cachaça

¼ teaspoon coarse sea salt

⅛ teaspoon freshly ground black pepper

INSTRUCTIONS

1. Combine all the ingredients in a bowl. Mix well.

Dulce de Leche

Yield: 1 cup dulce de leche

INGREDIENT

One 14-ounce can sweetened condensed milk

INSTRUCTIONS

1. Position a rack in the center of the oven and preheat to 425°F.

2. Place the condensed milk in an 8-inch square baking pan.

3. Cover the pan tightly with tinfoil and place in a large baking or roasting pan.

4. Pour boiling water halfway up the outsides of the milk pan.

5. Bake until the mixture is thick and caramel brown, about 1 ¼ hours. Maintain the level of water in the larger pan by adding more water, if necessary, as the milk bakes.

6. Remove the milk pan from the water bath, uncover the pan, and place it on a wire rack to cool completely.

Note

Store in an airtight container in the fridge for up to 2 weeks. Bring to room temperature before using.

Bourbon Whipped Cream

Yield: 3 cups whipped cream

Note

Refrigerate until ready to use. Whipped cream can be made up to 6 hours in advance and will keep for up to 2 days in the fridge, though it will start to lose some of its airiness the longer it sits.

INGREDIENTS

1 cup heavy cream

2 tablespoons bourbon whiskey

2 tablespoons pure maple syrup

1 teaspoon pure vanilla extract

INSTRUCTIONS

1. Place your mixing bowl and paddles (or beaters, if using an electric hand mixer) in the fridge. The colder you keep your tools and ingredients, the easier the whipped cream will form.

2. When ready to make the cream, pour the cream in the chilled bowl. Whip at high speed until soft peaks form in a stand mixer fitted with the paddle attachment. Be mindful not to overwhip, or you'll end up with butter.

3. Add the bourbon whiskey, maple syrup, and vanilla.

Acknowledgments

So this book happened. And while I wrote the words on the pages and photographed the images, it wouldn't have been anything more than a dream if it weren't for the incredible team, brimming with love and support, that I'm fortunate enough to have on my side.

Thank you to my Editor at Countryman Press, Ann Treistman, for having faith in my artwork and ability. I know working with a first-time author isn't the easiest thing to do and you were exponentially gracious with your guidance. Thanks for creating order from my chaos—I'm so grateful that you took a chance on a book that can be as easily drunk as it is eaten.

Thank you, Nick Caruso, for your vision and generosity in working with me, and for creating a beautiful book. Your talent for putting it all together is astounding.

To my Publicist, Devorah Backman, I am forever grateful.

To the super-human recipe testers and editors who stuck with me for months and months and months: You amaze me. To commit so much to a project that isn't even yours, is beyond generous. This is our book. Thank you Becky Calvert, Blaine and Barb Willey, Camilla Mann, Denise Alonso, Fina Cardwell, Gayle McCleod, Gloria Duggan, Haydn Johnstone, Jane Craske, JoAnn Dragland, Kaitlyn Webb-Patience, Kathryn Geyer, Megan Band, Michele Eggert Phillips, Michelle Atkinson, Michelle and Kyle James, Momma Bear and Brother Bear, Renee Baude, Shane Johnson, Sharon Watt, and Shelby Redmond.

To the kindred spirits who inspired and helped me navigate the cocktail that is professional publishing: Gin, tequila, and bourbon. Jk, jk... Seriously though, thank you: Aimée Wimbush-Bourque, Amy Bronee, Carol Lovett, Charmian Christie, Ethan Adeland, Erin Scott, Jane Bonacci, Jenny Schacht, Julie Van Rosendall, and Melissa Hartfiel.

To the painfully talented woman who donated her Midnight collection for the book (featured on the cover), Gabrielle Burke of G Ceramic & Co—you are one of a kind. Much like your hand-made ceramics. They're stunning. And so is your soul. Thank you for making my life—and this book—more beautiful.

To my Editor at *Edible Vancouver* for forgiving my tardiness meeting deadlines while I created this book—Debbra Mikaelsen, you are a saint. Not to mention a damn fine writer.

To the people who read, comment, share, engage with, support, love, and cook recipes from *SheEats.ca*, or who have bought this book—I need you. So does my bourbon habit. Let's have one (or three) sometime.

To my family—I love you.

To my Mom, Michael, and Mauria—you're alright ;)

To my Dad—I miss you.

To my friends—you are the family I've chosen. And you're never getting away from me. Like it or not.

To Amber. Wives till the end. Or at least until the end of the bottle (or three). With all our dark and twisty places.

To Haydn—you make me laugh as much as you make me cry.

To Kaitlyn—your boldness makes me more honest.

To Kendra—you have relentless love and I'm fortunate to be on the receiving end of that.

To Krista—you kick my ass. In a good way.

To Shelby—your shoe fashion sense is inspiring. And so are you.

To just a few of the fiercely talented people who make my life better: All the folks in the Food Bloggers of Canada community, Amy Ruth (for your endless adventure), Bill Carroll (for pulling back the curtain), Christine St Peter (for inspiring all of this from the very beginning and teaching me so many things—including how to have a voice and accomplish what I want in life), Darina Kopcok (for shared sensibilities over lunch), Gabby Gott (for living your truth through and through), Jayme Marie Henderson (for sending care packages when I need them most), Julie Kotzbach (for your talent), Mike Deitch (for shrubs and your affinity for whiskey), Mairlyn Smith (for your bravery), Suzie Durigon (for being a kindred in humor), Lindsey Nickell (for your friendship), Meghan McCarthy (for reminding me what badass looks like), Michelle Moore (for seeing all the beauty and inspiring me), Samantha Mosher (for living my dream life... in Brooklyn), Sean Bromilow (for all the things you know), Stacey Davidson (for everything), and Suzanne Smith Collier (for making me laugh).

To the thirst quenchers who make my life better (none of them have paid me to say this—but they should, wink wink): Burrowing Owl Estate Winery, Casamigos Tequila, Four Roses Bourbon, Le Vieux Pin Winery, Odd Society Spirits, The Liberty Distillery, Phillips Brewing & Malting Co, Victoria Gin, and Woodford Reserve.

To those who turn my world upside down: Amy Schumer (can we please drink wine—I'll buy!), Ani Difranco (you speak to my heart-soul), The Counting Crows (you keep my company), *Friends* (yes, the TV show), Julia Child (more butter, please), Maya Rudolph (I admit my dreams), Raj Patel (your work is valuable), Rosemary Hennessy (mind blown), Stephen King (adverbs are the devil), Yann Martel (all the adventure and important things), and anything that's aired on AMC. Ever.

Lastly, thank you to the man I'm about to call my husband. For all his love and kindness when I was losing my shit, when I was in the shit, about all the shit. I'm so grateful you don't mind that I talk about poop all the time. And that you encourage me every single day to be myself without apology and make things happen. Including dreams like this book. Thank you.

Index

A

Acorn Squash, Radicchio & Lamb Merguez with Sweet Vermouth, Baked, 105–7
Ale-Battered Fish (no chips), 140–41
Ale Stacked Mushrooms, 160–61
Amarula Cookies, Grandma's Chocolate Chip, 192–93
appetizers & bar snacks, 58–79
    Brandy-Laced Chicken Liver Pâté, 72–73
    Cheese & Rum Marinated Pineapple Sticks, 68–69
    Crunchy Pommes Frites with Madeira Balsamic Reduction, 76–77
    Estrella Jamón & Croquettes, 62–63
    "Fundo" Pull-Apart Bread, 70–71
    Limoncello Shrimp with Black Pepper & Mango Salsa, 64–65
    Red Wine Chorizo with Blistered Cherry Tomatoes & Fresh Herbs, 66–67
    Strawberry Chambord Whipped Stilton Cheese Toasts, 60–61
    Verdejo Habas con Jamón (Fava Beans with Spanish Ham & Wine), 78–79
    Vodka-Spiked Butternut Squash "Parcels" & Bloody Mary Tomato Jam, 74–75
apples
    Apple Cider Pound Cake, 178–79
    Apple Cider Roasted Pork Loin, 108–10
    Cinnamon Apple Whiskey Sour, 54–55
asparagus
    Mezcal Pan Asparagus & Perfect Poached Eggs, 158–59
    Parchment-Baked Grappa Halibut "Cocktail," 126–27

avocados
    Cachaça Grilled Avocado with Cachaça Condiments, 174–75
    Fiesta Boozy Guac, 232
    Mango Salsa, 233

B

bacon
    "Fundo" Pull-Apart Bread, 70–71
    JD Mac & Peas, 152–54
    Maple Bacon Bourbon Manhattan with Bacon Salt, 48–49
    Mom's Stout Baked Beans, 164–65
    Sparkling Rosé Roquefort Wedge Salad, 94–95
    See also pancetta
Baileys Irish Cream, in Dirty Sexy Coffee Drinks (a.k.a. Shafts), 44–45
Baked Beans, Mom's Stout, 164–65
Balsamic Reduction, Madeira Wine, 221
Balsamicy Onions, 219
barley
    Beef & Barley Red Wine Stew, 92–93
    IPA Curried Barley Vegeta-bowls, 168–70
bar snacks. See appetizers & bar snacks
BBQ Sauce, Smoky Stout or Maple Whiskey, 227
beans and legumes
    black beans, in St. Rita Quesadillas, 162–63
    lentils, in Martini Puttanesca & Seared Salmon, 136–37
    Mom's Stout Baked Beans, 164–65

beans and legumes (*continued*)

Verdejo Habas con Jamón (Fava Beans with Spanish Ham & Wine), 78–79

beef

Beef & Barley Red Wine Stew, 92–93

Grilled Flank Steak with Bordelaise Sauce, 118–19

Maple Whiskey-Laced BBQ Meatballs, 116–17

Rob Roy Braised Short Ribs, 122–23

beer

Ale-Battered Fish (no chips), 140–41

Ale Stacked Mushrooms, 160–61

Chocolate Porter-Marinated Lamb Pops with Pea, Mint, & Feta "Salad," 114–15

Cuervo & Tecate Pork Carnitas, 100–101

Estrella Jamón & Croquettes, 62–63

"Fundo" Pull-Apart Bread, 70–71

IPA Curried Barley Vegeta-bowls, 168–70

Lager-Simmered Chicken Thighs, 120–21

Mom's Stout Baked Beans, 164–65

Smoky Stout or Maple Whiskey BBQ Sauce, 227

Stout Blue Cheese Bison Burgers, 105–7

beets

Boozy Beet Shrub, 52–53

IPA Curried Barley Vegeta-bowls, 168–70

Beignets with Sambuca Coffee Crème Anglaise, Fried, 180–82

Bison Burgers, Stout Blue Cheese, 102–4

Bitter Wilted Greens, Grappa Ricotta Gnocchi with, 166–67

Bloody Mary Tomato Jam, 220

Bloody Mary Tomato Jam, Vodka-Spiked Butternut Squash "Parcels" &, 74–75

Blueberry Crisp, Peach Schnapps, 196–97

Blue Cheese Bison Burgers, Stout, 102–4

Boozy Beet Shrub, 52–53

Boozy Ice Cream, 3-Way, 198–201

Bordelaise Sauce, 229

Bordelaise Sauce, Grilled Flank Steak with, 118–19

Boulevardier, 34–35

bourbon whiskey

Boulevardier, 34–35

Bourbon-Soaked Cherries, 216–17

Bourbon-Soaked Cherries Tiramisu, 190–91

Bourbon Whipped Cream, 236

in chocolate mint julep (ice cream) variation, 200

Cinnamon Apple Whiskey Sour, 54–55

Maple Bacon Bourbon Manhattan with Bacon Salt, 48–49

"Old-Fashioned" Pumpkin Pots de Crème, 204–5

Brandy-Laced Chicken Liver Pâté, 72–73

Brandy Melt, Smoked Trout, 142–43

Bread, "Fundo" Pull-Apart, 70–71

Bread Pudding, Crispy Crunch, 194–95

Brie Salad, Drunk Grilled Pear &, 82–83

Brownies & Ganache, Raspberry Vodka, 202–3

Brussels Sprout & Mushroom Risotto, Sauvignon Blanc, 171–73

Burgers, Stout Blue Cheese Bison, 102–4

Buttercream Frosting, Layered Naked Champagne Cake with, 208–10

Butternut Squash "Parcels" & Bloody Mary Tomato Jam, Vodka-Spiked, 74–75

C

cachaça

Cachaça Grilled Avocado with Cachaça Condiments, 174–75

Cachaça Lime Sauce, 233

Cachaça Salsa Fresca, 234

Caesar, Snackin', 50–51

cake(s)

Apple Cider Pound Cake, 178–79

Layered Naked Champagne, with Butter-
cream Frosting, 208–10
cauliflower
Cauliflower, Kale, & Grapefruit Salad,
86–87
Gewürztraminer Thai Mussels, 130–32
IPA Curried Barley Vegeta-bowls, 168–70
Cazuelitas de Bacalao, Chardonnay, 147–49
celery salt, in Snackin' Caesar, 50–51
Ceviche!, One Tequila, Two Tequila, Three
Tequila, 138–39
Chambord liqueur, in Strawberry Chambord
Whipped Stilton Cheese Toasts, 60–61
Champagne Cake with Buttercream Frosting,
Layered Naked, 208–10
Chardonnay Cazuelitas de Bacalao, 147–49
cheddar cheese
"Fundo" Pull-Apart Bread, 70–71
JD Mac & Peas, 152–54
St. Rita Quesadillas, 162–63
cheese
& Rum Marinated Pineapple Sticks,
68–69
smoked, in St. Rita Quesadillas, 162–63
Wine and Cheese Plate, 211–13
See also specific cheeses
Cheesecake, Classic NY-Style Margarita,
188–89
Cherries, Bourbon-Soaked, 216–17
Cherries Tiramisu, Bourbon-Soaked, 190–91
Chicken Liver Pâté, Brandy-Laced, 72–73
Chicken Thighs, Lager-Simmered, 120–21
chile peppers
Cachaça Salsa Fresca, 234
Cuervo & Tecate Pork Carnitas, 100–101
Gewürztraminer Thai Mussels, 130–32
One Tequila, Two Tequila, Three Tequila,
Ceviche!, 138–39
Sake to Me Scallops, 133–35
St. Rita Quesadillas, 162–63

chocolate
chocolate mint julep (ice cream) variation,
200
Chocolate Porter-Marinated Lamb Pops
with Pea, Mint, & Feta "Salad," 114–15
Grandma's Chocolate Chip Amarula Cook-
ies, 192–93
Grilled Salted Dulce de Leche Chocolate
Kahlúa Coffee Sandwiches, 206–7
Raspberry Vodka Brownies & Ganache,
202–3
Cinnamon Apple Whiskey Sour, 54–55
Clamato juice, in Snackin' Caesar, 50–51
Clams, Dry Vermouth Drunken, 128–29
cocktails, 32–57
Boozy Beet Shrub, 52–53
Boulevardier, 34–35
Cinnamon Apple Whiskey Sour, 54–55
Classic Lime Daiquiri, 40–41
Dirty Sexy Coffee Drinks, 44–45
Elderflower Summer Spritz, 42–43
French 75 2.0, 38–39
Maple Bacon Bourbon Manhattan with
Bacon Salt, 48–49
Mint Cucumber & Smoky Jalapeño Margar-
ita, 42–43
"Moscow" Dark & Stormy, 36–37
Rhuby-Tom, 46–47
Snackin' Caesar, 50–51
cod, in Chardonnay Cazuelitas de Bacalao,
147–49
coffee
Bourbon-Soaked Cherries Tiramisu,
190–91
Dirty Sexy Coffee Drinks (a.k.a. Shafts),
44–45
Sambuca Coffee Crème Anglaise, Fried
Beignets with, 180–82
Cointreau, in Mint Cucumber & Smoky Jala-
peño Margarita, 42–43

Compari liqueur, in Boulevardier, 34–35

Cookies, Grandma's Chocolate Chip Amarula, 192–93

cream cheese, in Classic NY-Style Margarita Cheesecake, 188–89

crème de cacao, in Crispy Crunch Bread Pudding, 194–95

Crème de Pamplemousse Rose (grapefruit) liqueur, in Cauliflower, Kale, & Grapefruit Salad, 86–87

Crispy Crunch Bread Pudding, 194–95

Croquettes, Estrella Jamón &, 62–63

crostini

Strawberry Chambord Whipped Stilton Cheese Toasts, 60–61

cucumbers, in Mint Cucumber & Smoky Jalapeño Margarita, 42–43

Cuervo & Tecate Pork Carnitas, 100–101

Curried Barley Vegeta-bowls, IPA, 168–70

custard desserts

"Old-Fashioned" Pumpkin Pots de Crème, 204–5

D

Daiquiri, Classic Lime, 40–41

Dark and Stormy Kettle Corn, 183–85

desserts. See sweets

Dirty Sexy Coffee Drinks (a.k.a. Shafts), 44–45

Drunk Grilled Pear & Brie Salad, 82–83

Drunk Pear Salad Dressing, 221

Dulce de Leche, 235

Dulce de Leche Chocolate Kahlúa Coffee Sandwiches, Grilled Salted, 206–7

E

Eggs, Mezcal Pan Asparagus & Perfect Poached, 158–59

Elderflower Summer Spritz, 42–43

equipment and tools, 22–31

Estrella Jamón & Croquettes, 62–63

F

Fava Beans with Spanish Ham & Wine (Verdejo Habas con Jamón), 78–79

feta cheese, in Mojito Watermelon Chopped Salad, 90–91

Fiesta Boozy Guac, 232

fish & seafood, 124–49

Ale-Battered Fish (no chips), 140–41

Chardonnay Cazuelitas de Bacalao, 147–49

Dry Vermouth Drunken Clams, 128–29

Gewürztraminer Thai Mussels, 130–32

Martini Puttanesca & Seared Salmon, 136–37

One Tequila, Two Tequila, Three Tequila, Ceviche!, 138–39

Parchment-Baked Grappa Halibut "Cocktail," 126–27

Sake to Me Scallops, 133–35

Smoked Trout & Brandy Melt, 142–43

Sparkling Panzanella Tuna Niçoise, 144–46

See also Limoncello Shrimp

Flank Steak with Bordelaise Sauce, Grilled, 118–19

Frangelico, in Crispy Crunch Bread Pudding, 194–95

French 75 2.0, 38–39

French Onion Soup, Irish Whiskey, 96–97

Frosting, Buttercream, 208, 210

fruit. See specific fruits

"Fundo" Pull-Apart Bread, 70–71

G

Ganache, Raspberry Vodka Brownies &, 202–3

garlic, in Sangria Ajo Blanco (Spanish White Garlic Soup), 88–89

Gewürztraminer Thai Mussels, 130–32

gin
    Boozy Beet Shrub, 52–53
    French 75 2.0, 38–39
    Martini Puttanesca & Seared Salmon,
        136–37
    Rhuby-Tom (Rhubarb Tom Collins), 46–47
    Snackin' Caesar, 50–51
    & tonic (ice cream) variation, 200
ginger beer
    Dark and Stormy Kettle Corn, 183–85
    "Moscow" Dark & Stormy, 36–37
Gnocchi with Bitter Wilted Greens, Grappa
        Ricotta, 166–67
goat cheese, in Ale Stacked Mushrooms,
        160–61
Grandma's Chocolate Chip Amarula Cookies,
        192–93
grapefruit liqueur (Crème de Pamplemousse
        Rose), in Cauliflower, Kale, & Grapefruit
        Salad, 86–87
Grapefruit Salad, Cauliflower, Kale, &, 86–87
grappa
    Grappa Ricotta Gnocchi with Bitter Wilted
        Greens, 166–67
    Parchment-Baked Grappa Halibut "Cock-
        tail," 126–27
green beans, in Sparkling Panzanella Tuna
        Niçoise, 144–46
Gruyère cheese
    "Fundo" Pull-Apart Bread, 70–71
    Irish Whiskey French Onion Soup, 96–97
    JD Mac & Peas, 152–54

H

halibut, in Parchment-Baked Grappa Halibut
        "Cocktail," 126–27
ham
    Drunk Grilled Pear & Brie Salad, 82–83
    Estrella Jamón & Croquettes, 62–63

Verdejo Habas con Jamón (Fava Beans with
        Spanish Ham & Wine), 78–79
    See also prosciutto
Herby Yogurt Sauce, 226
Homemade Stock, 224

I

Ice Cream, 3-Way Boozy, 198–201
ingredients, essential, 19–22
IPA Curried Barley Vegeta-bowls, 168–70
Irish Whiskey French Onion Soup, 96–97

J

jalapeño peppers, in Mint Cucumber & Smoky
        Jalapeño Margarita, 42–43
Jam, Bloody Mary Tomato, 220
JD Mac & Peas, 152–54

K

Kahlúa
    Bourbon-Soaked Cherries Tiramisu, 190–91
    Dirty Sexy Coffee Drinks (a.k.a. Shafts), 44–45
    Grilled Salted Dulce de Leche Chocolate
        Kahlúa Coffee Sandwiches, 206–7
Kale, & Grapefruit Salad, Cauliflower, 86–87
kale, in IPA Curried Barley Vegeta-bowls, 168–70
Kettle Corn, Dark and Stormy, 183–85
kitchen tools and equipment, 22–31

L

Lager-Simmered Chicken Thighs, 120–21
lamb
    Baked Acorn Squash, Radicchio, & Lamb
        Merguez with Sweet Vermouth, 105–7
    Chocolate Porter-Marinated Lamb Pops
        with Pea, Mint, & Feta "Salad," 114–15

Layered Naked Champagne Cake with Butter-
    cream Frosting, 208–10
lemongrass, in Sake to Me Scallops, 133–35
lentils, in Martini Puttanesca & Seared Salmon,
    136–37
limes
    Cachaça Lime Sauce, 233
    Lime Daiquiri, Classic, 40–41
    limes, in Dark and Stormy Kettle Corn, 183–
    85
limoncello, in French 75 2.0, 38–39
Limoncello Shrimp with Black Pepper &
    Mango Salsa, 64–65
liqueurs. See specific liqueurs

M

Madeira Balsamic Reduction, Crunchy Pom-
    mes Frites with, 76–77
Madeira Wine Balsamic Reduction, 221
Mango Salsa, 233
Mango Salsa, Limoncello Shrimp with Black
    Pepper &, 64–65
Manhattan with Bacon Salt, Maple Bacon
    Bourbon, 48–49
maple syrup
    Maple Bacon Bourbon Manhattan with
    Bacon Salt, 48–49
    Maple Whiskey BBQ Sauce, 227
    Maple Whiskey-Laced BBQ Meatballs,
    116–17
    "Old-Fashioned" Pumpkin Pots de Crème,
    204–5
Margarita, Mint Cucumber & Smoky Jalapeño,
    42–43
Margarita Cheesecake, Classic NY-Style,
    188–89
Margarita Tomato Sauce, 231
Margherita "Margarita" Pizza, 155–57
Martini Puttanesca & Seared Salmon, 136–37

mascarpone cheese, in Bourbon-Soaked Cher-
    ries Tiramisu, 190–91
Meatballs, Maple Whiskey-Laced BBQ, 116–17
meats, 98–123
    Apple Cider Roasted Pork Loin, 108–10
    Baked Acorn Squash, Radicchio & Lamb
    Merguez with Sweet Vermouth, 105–7
    Chocolate Porter-Marinated Lamb Pops
    with Pea, Mint, & Feta "Salad," 114–15
    Cuervo & Tecate Pork Carnitas, 100–101
    Grilled Flank Steak with Bordelaise Sauce,
    118–19
    Lager-Simmered Chicken Thighs, 120–21
    Maple Whiskey-Laced BBQ Meatballs, 116–17
    Rob Roy Braised Short Ribs, 122–23
    Sherry Ragu with Rabbit & Pappardelle
    Noodles, 111–13
    Stout Blue Cheese Bison Burgers, 102–4
    See also specific meats
Mezcal Pan Asparagus & Perfect Poached
    Eggs, 158–59
Mint Cucumber & Smoky Jalapeño Margarita,
    42–43
Mojito Watermelon Chopped Salad, 90–91
Mojito Watermelon Salad Dressing, 219, 222
Mom's Stout Baked Beans, 164–65
"Moscow" Dark & Stormy, 36–37
mozzarella cheese, in Margherita "Margarita"
    Pizza, 155–57
mushrooms
    Ale Stacked Mushrooms, 160–61
    Mushroom Thyme Sherry Soup, 84–85
    Sauvignon Blanc Brussels Sprout & Mush-
    room Risotto, 171–73
Mussels, Gewürztraminer Thai, 130–32

N

NY-Style Margarita Cheesecake, Classic,
    188–89

O

"Old-Fashioned" Pumpkin Pots de Crème, 204–5

One Tequila, Two Tequila, Three Tequila, Ceviche!, 138–39

onions
  Balsamicy, 219
  Irish Whiskey French Onion Soup, 96–97
  Quick Pickled, 228

orange liqueur
  Bourbon-Soaked Cherries Tiramisu, 190–91
  Classic NY-Style Margarita Cheesecake, 188–89

P

pancetta, in Pan Asparagus & Perfect Poached Eggs, 158–59

pantry essentials, 19–22

Panzanella Tuna Niçoise, Panzanella, 144–46

parmesan cheese, in Sauvignon Blanc Brussels Sprout & Mushroom Risotto, 171–73

pasta and noodles
  JD Mac & Peas, 152–54
  Sherry Ragu with Rabbit & Pappardelle Noodles, 111–13

Pâté, Brandy-Laced Chicken Liver, 72–73

Peach Schnapps Blueberry Crisp, 196–97

pear(s)
  Drunk Grilled Pear & Brie Salad, 82–83
  liqueur, in Drunk Pear Salad Dressing, 221
  Spanish Wine-Poached, 186–87

Peas, JD Mac &, 152–54

peppers, hot. See chile peppers

Pickled Onions, Quick, 225

Pineapple Sticks, Cheese & Rum Marinated, 68–69

Pizza, Margherita "Margarita," 155–57

Polenta, Classic, 230

Pommes Frites with Madeira Balsamic Reduction, Crunchy, 76–77

popcorn
  Dark and Stormy Kettle Corn, 183–85

pork
  Apple Cider Roasted Pork Loin, 108–10
  Cuervo & Tecate Pork Carnitas, 100–101
  ground, in Maple Whiskey-Laced BBQ Meatballs, 116–17
  sausage, in Red Wine Chorizo with Blistered Cherry Tomatoes & Fresh Herbs, 66–67
  See also bacon; ham

potatoes
  Chardonnay Cazuelitas de Bacalao, 147–49
  Pommes Frites with Madeira Balsamic Reduction, Crunchy, 76–77
  Sparkling Panzanella Tuna Niçoise, 144–46

Pots de Crème, "Old-Fashioned" Pumpkin, 204–5

Pound Cake, Apple Cider, 178–79

prosciutto, in Drunk Grilled Pear & Brie Salad, 82–83

Pumpkin Pots de Crème, "Old Fashioned," 204–5

Puttanesca & Seared Salmon, Martini, 136–37

Q

Quesadillas, St. Rita, 162–63

R

Rabbit & Pappardelle Noodles, Sherry Ragu with, 111–13

Raspberry Vodka Brownies & Ganache, 202–3

Red Wine Chorizo with Blistered Cherry Tomatoes & Fresh Herbs, 66–67

Rhuby-Tom (Rhubarb Tom Collins), 46–47

rice, in Sauvignon Blanc Brussels Sprout & Mushroom Risotto, 171–73

ricotta cheese

Grappa Ricotta Gnocchi with Bitter Wilted Greens, 166–67

Vodka-Spiked Butternut Squash "Parcels" & Bloody Mary Tomato Jam, 74–75

Risotto, Sauvignon Blanc Brussels Sprout & Mushroom, 171–73

Rob Roy Braised Short Ribs, 122–23

roquefort cheese

Sparkling Rosé Roquefort Salad Dressing, 223

Sparkling Rosé Roquefort Wedge Salad, 94–95

rum

Cheese & Rum Marinated Pineapple Sticks, 68–69

Classic Lime Daiquiri, 40–41

Dark and Stormy Kettle Corn, 183–85

"Moscow" Dark & Stormy, 34–35, 36–37

pralines, rum & caramel (ice cream) variation, 200–201

S

Sake to Me Scallops, 133–35

salad dressings

Drunk Pear, 221

Mojito Watermelon, 222

Sparkling Rosé Roquefort, 223

salad(s)

Cauliflower, Kale, & Grapefruit, 86–87

Drunk Grilled Pear & Brie, 82–83

Mojito Watermelon Chopped Salad, 90–91

Sparkling Rosé Roquefort Wedge, 94–95

salmon, in Martini Puttanesca & Seared Salmon, 136–37

Salsa, Mango, 233

Salsa Fresca, Cachaça, 234

Salted Dulce de Leche Chocolate Kahlúa Coffee Sandwiches, Grilled, 206–7

Sambuca Coffee Crème Anglaise, 180–82

Sandwiches, Grilled Salted Dulce de Leche Chocolate Kahlúa Coffee, 206–7

Sangria Ajo Blanco (Spanish White Garlic Soup), 88–89

sauces. See staples & sauces

sausage

Baked Acorn Squash, Radicchio & Lamb Merguez with Sweet Vermouth, 105–7

Red Wine Chorizo with Blistered Cherry Tomatoes & Fresh Herbs, 66–67

Sauvignon Blanc Brussels Sprout & Mushroom Risotto, 171–73

Scallops, Sake to Me, 133–35

scotch whiskey, in Rob Roy Braised Short Ribs, 122–23

seafood. See fish & seafood

Shafts. See Dirty Sexy Coffee Drinks (a.k.a. Shafts)

sherry, in Mushroom Thyme Sherry Soup, 84–85

Sherry Ragu with Rabbit & Pappardelle Noodles, 111–13

Shrub, Boozy Beet, 52–53

Simple Syrup, 218

Smoked Trout & Brandy Melt, 142–43

Smoky Stout or Maple Whiskey BBQ Sauce, 227

Snackin' Caesar, 50–51

soups & salads, 80–97

Beef & Barley Red Wine Stew, 92–93

Cauliflower, Kale, & Grapefruit Salad, 86–87

Drunk Grilled Pear & Brie Salad, 82–83

Irish Whiskey French Onion Soup, 96–97

Mojito Watermelon Chopped Salad, 90–91

Mushroom Thyme Sherry Soup, 84–85

soups & salads (*continued*)

Sangria Ajo Blanco (Spanish White Garlic Soup), 88–89

Sparkling Rosé Roquefort Wedge Salad, 94–95

Spanish White Garlic Soup (Sangria Ajo Blanco), 88–89

Spanish Wine-Poached Pears, 186–87

Sparkling Panzanella Tuna Niçoise, 144–46

Sparkling Rosé Roquefort Salad Dressing, 223

Sparkling Rosé Roquefort Wedge Salad, 94–95

squash

Baked Acorn Squash, Radicchio & Lamb Merguez with Sweet Vermouth, 105–7

Butternut Squash "Parcels" & Bloody Mary Tomato Jam, Vodka-Spiked, 74–75

sriracha hot sauce, in Snackin' Caesar, 50–51

staples & sauces, 214–39

Balsamicy Onions, 219

Bloody Mary Tomato Jam, 220

Bordelaise Sauce, 229

Bourbon Soaked Cherries, 216–17

Bourbon Whipped Cream, 236

Cachaça Lime Sauce, 233

Cachaça Salsa Fresca, 234

Classic Polenta, 230

Drunk Pear Salad Dressing, 221

Dulce de Leche, 235

Fiesta Boozy Guac, 232

Herby Yogurt Sauce, 226

Homemade Stock, 224

Madeira Wine Balsamic Reduction, 221

Mango Salsa, 233

Margarita Tomato Sauce, 231

Mojito Watermelon Salad Dressing, 222

Quick Pickled Onions, 228

Simple Syrup, 218

Smoky Stout or Maple Whiskey BBQ Sauce, 227

Sparkling Rosé Roquefort Salad Dressing, 223

Spiced Yogurt Sauce, 225

Stew, Beef & Barley Red Wine, 92–93

St-Germain liqueur

Elderflower Summer Spritz, 42–43

Fiesta Boozy Guac, 232

Sangria Ajo Blanco (Spanish White Garlic Soup), 88–89

St. Rita Quesadillas, 162–63

Stilton cheese, in Strawberry Chambord Whipped Stilton Cheese Toasts, 60–61

Stock, Homemade, 224

Stout Blue Cheese Bison Burgers, 102–4

Strawberry Chambord Whipped Stilton Cheese Toasts, 60–61

St. Rita Quesadillas, 162–63

sweetened condensed milk, in Dulce de Leche, 235

sweet potatoes, in IPA Curried Barley Vegeta-bowls, 168–70

sweets, 176–213

Beignets with Sambuca Coffee Crème Anglaise, Fried, 180–82

Blueberry Crisp, Peach Schnapps, 196–97

Bread Pudding, Crispy Crunch, 194–95

Brownies & Ganache, Raspberry Vodka, 202–3

Champagne Cake with Buttercream Frosting, Layered Naked, 208–10

Cheesecake, Classic NY-Style Margarita, 188–89

Cookies, Grandma's Chocolate Chip Amarula, 192–93

Dulce de Leche Chocolate Kahlúa Coffee Sandwiches, Grilled Salted, 206–7

Ice Cream, 3-Way Boozy, 198–201

Kettle Corn, Dark and Stormy, 183–85

Pears, Spanish Wine-Poached, 186–87

Pots de Crème, "Old Fashioned" Pumpkin, 204–5

Pound Cake, Apple Cider, 178–79

Tiramisu, Bourbon-Soaked Cherries, 190–91

Swiss chard, in Gewürztraminer Thai Mussels, 130–32

T

tequila
  Classic NY-Style Margarita Cheesecake, 188–89
  Fiesta Boozy Guac, 232
  Mint Cucumber & Smoky Jalapeño Margarita, 42–43
  One Tequila, Two Tequila, Three Tequila, Ceviche!, 138–39
Thai Mussels, Gewürztraminer, 130–32
3-Way Boozy Ice Cream, 198–201
Tiramisu, Bourbon-Soaked Cherries, 190–91
tomatoes
  Blistered Cherry Tomatoes & Fresh Herbs, Red Wine Chorizo with, 66–67
  Bloody Mary Tomato Jam, 220
  Cachaça Salsa Fresca, 234
  Margarita Tomato Sauce, 231
  Parchment-Baked Grappa Halibut "Cocktail," 126–27
Tom Collins. See Rhuby-Tom (Rhubarb Tom Collins)
tools and equipment, 22–31
Trout & Brandy Melt, Smoked, 142–43
Tuna Niçoise, Sparkling Panzanella, 144–46

V

vegetables, 150–75
  Ale Stacked Mushrooms, 160–61
  Cachaça Grilled Avocado with Cachaça Condiments, 174–75
  IPA Curried Barley Vegeta-bowls, 168–70
  JD Mac & Peas, 152–54
  Margherita "Margarita" Pizza, 155–57
  Mom's Stout Baked Beans, 164–65
  Sauvignon Blanc Brussels Sprout & Mushroom Risotto, 171–73
  St. Rita Quesadillas, 162–63
  See also specific vegetables

Verdejo Habas con Jamón (Fava Beans with Spanish Ham & Wine), 78–79
vermouth, dry
  Dry Vermouth Drunken Clams, 128–29
  Martini Puttanesca & Seared Salmon, 136–37
vermouth, sweet
  Baked Acorn Squash, Radicchio & Lamb Merguez with, 105–7
  Boulevardier, 34–35
  Maple Bacon Bourbon Manhattan with Bacon Salt, 48–49
  Rob Roy Braised Short Ribs, 122–23
vodka
  Bloody Mary Tomato Jam, 220
  Elderflower Summer Spritz, 42–43
  Raspberry Vodka Brownies & Ganache, 202–3
  -Spiked Butternut Squash "Parcels" & Bloody Mary Tomato Jam, 74–75

W

Watermelon Chopped Salad, Mojito, 90–91
Whipped Cream, Bourbon, 236
whiskey
  Cinnamon Apple Whiskey Sour, 54–55
  JD Mac & Peas, 152–54
  Smoky Stout or Maple Whiskey BBQ Sauce, 227
  See also bourbon whiskey; scotch whiskey
wine
  Beef & Barley Red Wine Stew, 92–93
  Bordelaise Sauce, 229
  Chardonnay Cazuelitas de Bacalao, 147–49
  French 75 2.0, 38–39
  Gewürztraminer Thai Mussels, 130–32
  Madeira Wine Balsamic Reduction, 221
  Red Wine Chorizo with Blistered Cherry Tomatoes & Fresh Herbs, 66–67

Sangria Ajo Blanco (Spanish White Garlic Soup), 88–89
Spanish Wine-Poached Pears, 186–87
Verdejo Habas con Jamón (Fava Beans with Spanish Ham & Wine), 78–79
wine, sparkling
　　Layered Naked Champagne Cake with Buttercream Frosting, 208–10
　　Sparkling Panzanella Tuna Niçoise, 144–46

Sparkling Rosé Roquefort Salad Dressing, 223
Sparkling Rosé Roquefort Wedge Salad, 94–95
Wine & Cheese Plate, 211–13

Y

Yogurt Sauce, Herby, 226
Yogurt Sauce, Spiced, 225